I0763493

# My Reflection

A Journal for Living on Purpose

THE IMPOWER GROUP

# Table of Contents

# Introduction

Before you embark on this life-changing journey you're about to take, I want to tell you how proud I am of you. I know what you're thinking, "You don't even know me to be proud of me." But, I don't have to know you personally to understand that this book found you at this exact moment of your life for a reason. The fact that you're reading this tells me that you've been through some challenges in your life, and you're ready to take control of your circumstances.

I know you're tired of living your life by chance, and you're prepared to live your life by choice. No amount of trauma disqualifies you from being worthy, being happy, and being loved. You deserve the best of everything that life has to offer. As long as you're willing to take full responsibility for your life, claim your personal power, and do the work, it will be yours.

*My Reflection* was created to be a journal and workbook companion to the second edition of my book, *Poor Me to Soul Rich: Spiritual Currency for the Mind, Heart & Soul.* But even if you don't have the book yet, this journal is a powerful tool that could make this one of the most transformative seasons of your life.

A reflection is an image that you see when you look in a mirror. So when you're alone, standing in front of a mirror, there's only you and the image being reflected back at you. There aren't any comments, opinions, or critics. So, who and what is the image in the mirror? This journal is about discovering the true answer to that question.

I know that can sound like a scary undertaking and some people go their whole lives without ever feeling like they truly understand who they are. I'm not saying that it's easy to peel back all of those layers of pain, confusion, and trauma to reveal our naked truths. Still, it's a necessary journey for those who want to become the best version of themselves. I want you to find peace and confidence in the fact that no matter what you discover through this process, ultimately, what you see in the reflection will be up to you.

***How to use this Book***

In the following pages, you will find exercises that were designed to help you:

- Get clear about the specific things you want from your life.
- Be honest about where you are in your life right now.
- Discover what's been holding you back from getting to where you want to be.
- Determine the things that you need to let go of.
- Make informed daily decisions towards fulfillment in every area of your life.

The journal is divided into five (5) steps.

***Step 1***

*My Vision*

What do I want my life to look like and feel like? Who is the person you want to become?

***Step 2***

*My Present*

Where am I in my life right now? What are my current circumstances? What areas of my life do I lack?

***Step 3***

*My Suitcase*

What things do I need to start saying "no" to? What do I need to let go of to get to where I want to be? What are the things that are draining me?

***Step 4***

*My Reflections*

Here, you will explore your thoughts, feelings, and "aha moments" about specific reflections from my book Poor Me to Soul Rich and determine what actions you can take to improve particular areas of your life.

***Step 5***

*My Intentions*

This will be the section where you record your journal of daily intentions, gratitude, and experiences.

The best way to work through the journal and get the best results is to complete one step before going to the next one. The idea behind the way this journal is organized is to help you get clear about what you want and where you are currently so that as you discover new insights from the book, you'll be better prepared to make educated steps for long-lasting change.

Steps four and five will be done simultaneously. As you record your thoughts and feelings in the My Reflections section while reading Poor Me to Soul Rich, you'll be journaling your daily experiences in the My Intentions section.

As you go through this self-discovery journey, remember, there are no right or wrong answers. Just be honest. Allow yourself to be entirely in the moment. You're not worrying about the past or the future, but simply being in the here and now. This journey is all about you and no one else.

I honor you because this isn't an easy path to take. It takes tremendous courage to dig through parts of ourselves we've tried to forget. You have to be brave to peel back the layers you've put on to protect yourself. It takes an extraordinary person to travel the long road to not only discover your truth but to live it.

Remember to give yourself compassion and grace through this process, and I look forward to meeting the phenomenal person you're about to become.

# My Vision

# The Big Picture

The only way to where you want to be in your life is to know exactly what that place looks like. How else will you know when you're there? Having a clear vision for your life is the most powerful first step you can take to making it a reality. It isn't just about determining what you want; it's about defining who you want to be.

For this exercise, I want to remove all the limits! No settling for less than what you really want. Don't allow yourself to be defined by limitations set by others – or even yourself.

To help you organize your thoughts, I've broken down the exercise into what I call the **8 Divisions of an Abundant Life.** These divisions represent the most influential categories that contribute to a fulfilling and abundant life.

In each division, write down the limitless vision for your life. Of course, your vision should be genuine and sincere.

## Health and Fitness

Love Life and Intimacy

## Intellectual life and Personal growth

## Social life and Travel

# Leisure and Self-Care

# Business and Career

# Money and Finances

# The Best Day Ever

Now that we know what the ***Big Picture*** of your ideal life looks like, we're going to break it down to your daily life. This exercise will help you design your life based on what you want your every day to look like. The sum total of your days will be what ultimately defines your life experience.

Think of your life as a masterpiece painting and you're the artist. The ***Big Picture*** is the full, vibrant complete painting in a frame hanging over the mantle. The ***Best Day Ever*** represents each small section of the painting that eventually becomes that masterpiece.

Once you complete your ***Best Day Ever***, you'll not only know if your daily life is in ***alignment*** with your big picture, you'll be able to create more days that feel like the ***Best Day Ever.***

Here are some questions to help you think about what to include in your day.

How would your day look?

What kinds of food do you want to eat?

How do you want to feel?

What do you want to be doing?

How do you want to spend your time?

What do you want to create?

What places do you want to go to?

What experiences do you want to have?

What people do you want to spend time with?

What passions do you want to be fulfilling?

Every day is going to be unique, but if you can express what the Best Day Ever looks like for yourself, you can start to create your days to make that ideal a reality. Based on how you answered the questions, put it all together into a description of your Best Day Ever. You don't have to answer every question. Use the things that resonate with you. Remember, this is YOUR Best Day Ever.

*Tip: Start from the time you wake up and think through the morning, afternoon, and evening.*

# My Life List

In this exercise, you will list the things that you want to achieve and experience in your life. This list is usually referred to as a "bucket list." I call it a Life List because I want you to focus on creating the life experience and moments instead of a list of things to check off before you die. There's a reason why so many people's bucket list never gets completed. Most of the things that people write down, they don't actually believe they will do. It just sounds good to say.

That's why for this life, next to each item that you write down on your Life List, I want you to write down a goal date that you plan to achieve the item or have the experience.

# Achievements

Write down all of the things you want to achieve in your life - physically, financially, creativity, career, business, etc.

.................................................. I Will Achieve By .........................

.................................................. I Will Achieve By .........................

.................................................. I Will Achieve By .........................

.................................................. I Will Achieve By .........................

.................................................. I Will Achieve By .........................

.................................................. I Will Achieve By .........................

.................................................. I Will Achieve By .........................

.................................................. I Will Achieve By .........................

.................................................. I Will Achieve By .........................

.................................................. I Will Achieve By .........................

.................................................. I Will Achieve By .........................

.................................................. I Will Achieve By .........................

.................................................. I Will Achieve By .........................

.................................................. I Will Achieve By .........................

.................................................. I Will Achieve By .........................

# Experiences

Write down all of the things you want to experience in your life - travel, once-in-a-lifetime events, challenges, foods, etc.

.............................................. I Will Achieve By ........................

.............................................. I Will Achieve By ........................

.............................................. I Will Achieve By ........................

.............................................. I Will Achieve By ........................

.............................................. I Will Achieve By ........................

.............................................. I Will Achieve By ........................

.............................................. I Will Achieve By ........................

.............................................. I Will Achieve By ........................

.............................................. I Will Achieve By ........................

.............................................. I Will Achieve By ........................

.............................................. I Will Achieve By ........................

.............................................. I Will Achieve By ........................

.............................................. I Will Achieve By ........................

.............................................. I Will Achieve By ........................

.............................................. I Will Achieve By ........................

# Things I Want

This is the section where you can write down all of the material things you want in your life. There's absolutely nothing wrong with wanting nice things. It's all about knowing that your true value doesn't come from things or money. Don't be afraid to dream! Beside each item, write down the estimated cost of the item. The purpose of writing down the cost is to show you that many of the things that you want are more attainable than you may think. This exercise is also great for fueling your motivation.

| Item Name | Estimated Cost |
| --- | --- |
| ............................................................ | .............................. |
| ............................................................ | .............................. |
| ............................................................ | .............................. |
| ............................................................ | .............................. |
| ............................................................ | .............................. |
| ............................................................ | .............................. |
| ............................................................ | .............................. |
| ............................................................ | .............................. |
| ............................................................ | .............................. |
| ............................................................ | .............................. |
| ............................................................ | .............................. |
| ............................................................ | .............................. |
| ............................................................ | .............................. |
| ............................................................ | .............................. |
| ............................................................ | .............................. |
| ............................................................ | .............................. |
| ............................................................ | .............................. |
| ............................................................ | .............................. |
| ............................................................ | .............................. |
| ............................................................ | .............................. |

# Dream Bigger

I think that many times we run our dreams through a filter based on the limitations that we put on ourselves and our abilities. For this exercise, you're going to turn that filter off and brainstorm your biggest dreams. Set a timer for 10 - 15 minutes and just write. No dream is too big. If you find it difficult to think of anything, think about some of the people you idolize and think about why you admire them. That should help get your juices flowing. Another great tip is to go sit outside and write or put on your headphones and turn on some relaxing music. No need to overthink it. Let your inner-child take over and it will flow.

# My Present

# Self-Assessment

To get to the place you want to be in the most critical areas of your life, you first have to know where you are in your life right now. You will review a series of statements that pertain to your current lifestyle in **8 separate life categories.** We will examine factors such as health and fitness, love life, personal growth, and much more. You will answer how strongly you agree or disagree with each statement.

Once you finish assessing yourself, you'll **rate your current status** in that category based on your answers. Then you will have to **list three actions** that you could take immediately to increase your rating in that category.

# Health & Fitness

I am happy with the way my body looks.

Strongly Disagree Disagree Agree Strongly Agree

I have a defined exercise program.

Strongly Disagree Disagree Agree Strongly Agree

I stick to my exercise program diligently.

Strongly Disagree Disagree Agree Strongly Agree

I eat healthy foods most days.

Strongly Disagree Disagree Agree Strongly Agree

I'm not a smoker or heavy drinker (alcohol).

Strongly Disagree Disagree Agree Strongly Agree

I feel younger than my actual age.

Strongly Disagree Disagree Agree Strongly Agree

I consistently have high energy levels.

Strongly Disagree — Disagree — Agree — Strongly Agree

My current weight is ............... my goal weight is .............

On a scale of 1 - 10, how would you rate your current Health & Fitness?

1 2 3 4 5 6 7 8 9 10

Based on your ratings, what are three actions you can immediately take to move towards a 10 rating in this category?

1. ..........................................................................................
..........................................................................................
..........................................................................................
..........................................................................................

2. ..........................................................................................
..........................................................................................
..........................................................................................
..........................................................................................

3. ..........................................................................................
..........................................................................................
..........................................................................................
..........................................................................................

# Love Life & Intimacy

My partner and I have a great relationship

Strongly Disagree | Disagree | Agree | Strongly Agree

I have an excellent self-love relationship

Strongly Disagree | Disagree | Agree | Strongly Agree

We spend a lot of quality time together

Strongly Disagree | Disagree | Agree | Strongly Agree

I'm satisfied with our level of intimacy

Strongly Disagree | Disagree | Agree | Strongly Agree

We have a great friendship

Strongly Disagree | Disagree | Agree | Strongly Agree

I feel like I can talk to my partner about anything and everything

Strongly Disagree | Disagree | Agree | Strongly Agree

I focus enough energy on my partner's needs

Strongly Disagree | Disagree | Agree | Strongly Agree

I would characterize our relationship as happy

On a scale of 1 - 10, how would you rate your current Love Life & Intimacy?

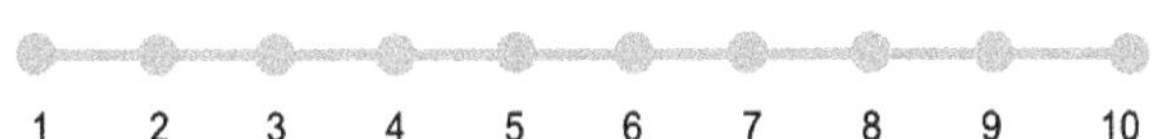


Based on your ratings, what are three actions you can immediately take to move towards a 10 rating in this category?

1. ..............................................................................................................
..............................................................................................................
..............................................................................................................
..............................................................................................................

2. ..............................................................................................................
..............................................................................................................
..............................................................................................................
..............................................................................................................

3. ..............................................................................................................
..............................................................................................................
..............................................................................................................
..............................................................................................................

# Intellectual Life & Personal Growth

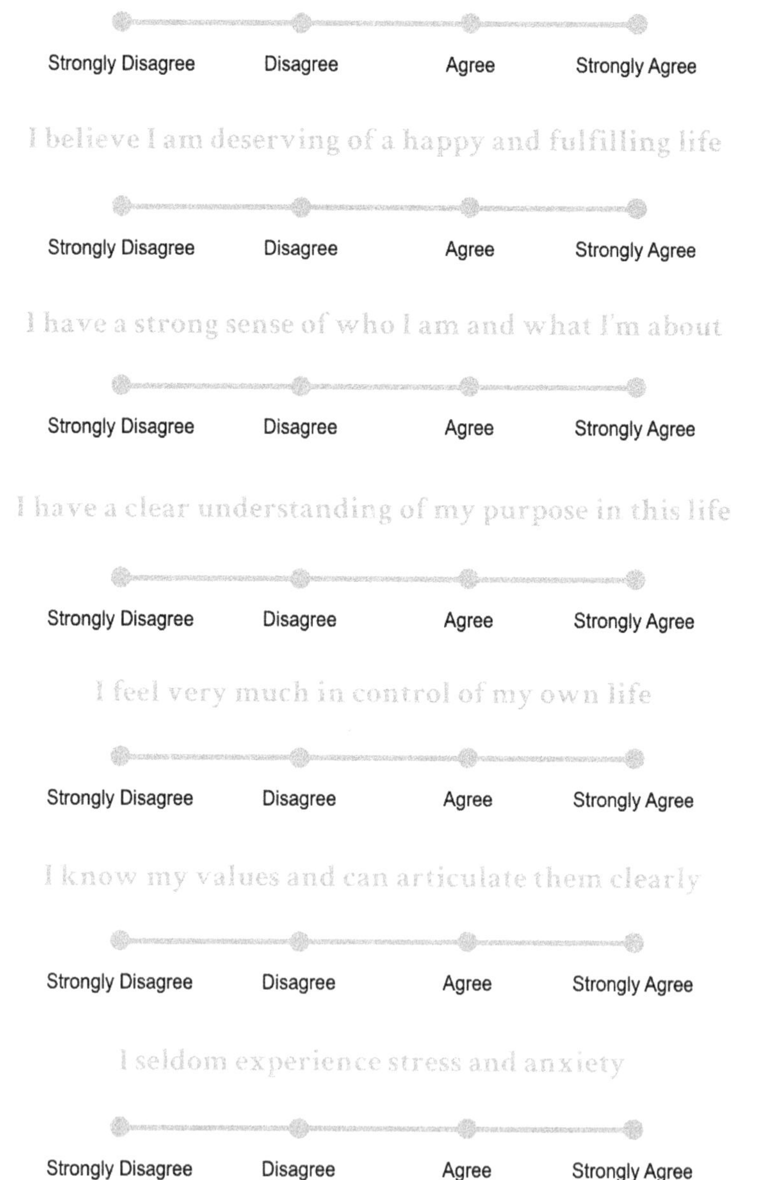

I dedicate a significant amount of time to learning and growing

Strongly Disagree | Disagree | Agree | Strongly Agree

I believe I am deserving of a happy and fulfilling life

Strongly Disagree | Disagree | Agree | Strongly Agree

I have a strong sense of who I am and what I'm about

Strongly Disagree | Disagree | Agree | Strongly Agree

I have a clear understanding of my purpose in this life

Strongly Disagree | Disagree | Agree | Strongly Agree

I feel very much in control of my own life

Strongly Disagree | Disagree | Agree | Strongly Agree

I know my values and can articulate them clearly

Strongly Disagree | Disagree | Agree | Strongly Agree

I seldom experience stress and anxiety

Strongly Disagree | Disagree | Agree | Strongly Agree

It's easy for me to express my emotions and how I feel

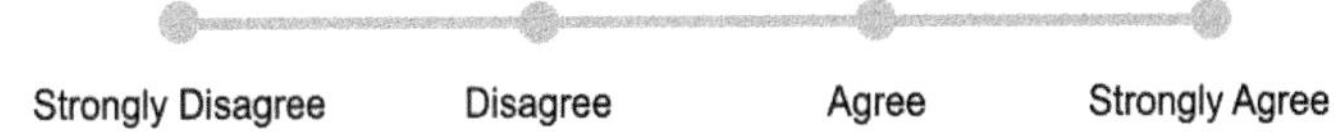


On a scale of 1 - 10, how would you rate your current Intellectual Life & Personal Growth?

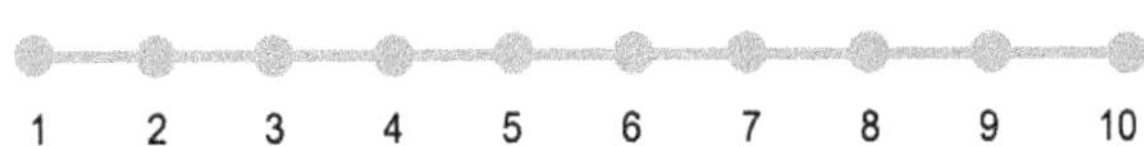


Based on your ratings, what are three actions you can immediately take to move towards a 10 rating in this category?

1. ..........................................................................................................
..........................................................................................................
..........................................................................................................
..........................................................................................................

2. ..........................................................................................................
..........................................................................................................
..........................................................................................................
..........................................................................................................

3. ..........................................................................................................
..........................................................................................................
..........................................................................................................
..........................................................................................................

# Family & Relationships

I have/had a close, loving, healthy relationship with my father

Strongly Disagree Disagree Agree Strongly Agree

I have/had a close, loving, healthy relationship with my mother

Strongly Disagree Disagree Agree Strongly Agree

I have/had a close, loving, healthy relationship with my siblings

Strongly Disagree Disagree Agree Strongly Agree

I invest a good deal of time and energy with my children

Strongly Disagree Disagree Agree Strongly Agree

I am happy with how my children are turning out as people

Strongly Disagree Disagree Agree Strongly Agree

My family and children are my #1 priority

Strongly Disagree Disagree Agree Strongly Agree

Overall, I feel like a great parent

Strongly Disagree Disagree Agree Strongly Agree

I set an excellent example for my children on how to be the best they can be

On a scale of 1 - 10, how would you rate your current Family & Relationships?

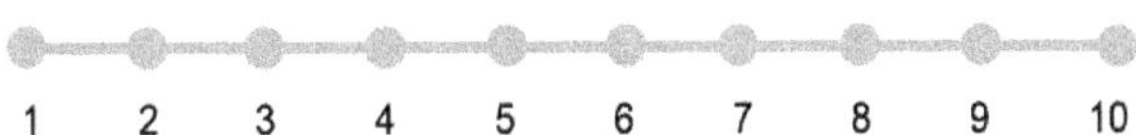


Based on your ratings, what are three actions you can immediately take to move towards a 10 rating in this category?

4. ............................................................................................................
............................................................................................................
............................................................................................................

5. ............................................................................................................
............................................................................................................
............................................................................................................

6. ............................................................................................................
............................................................................................................
............................................................................................................

# Social Life & Travel

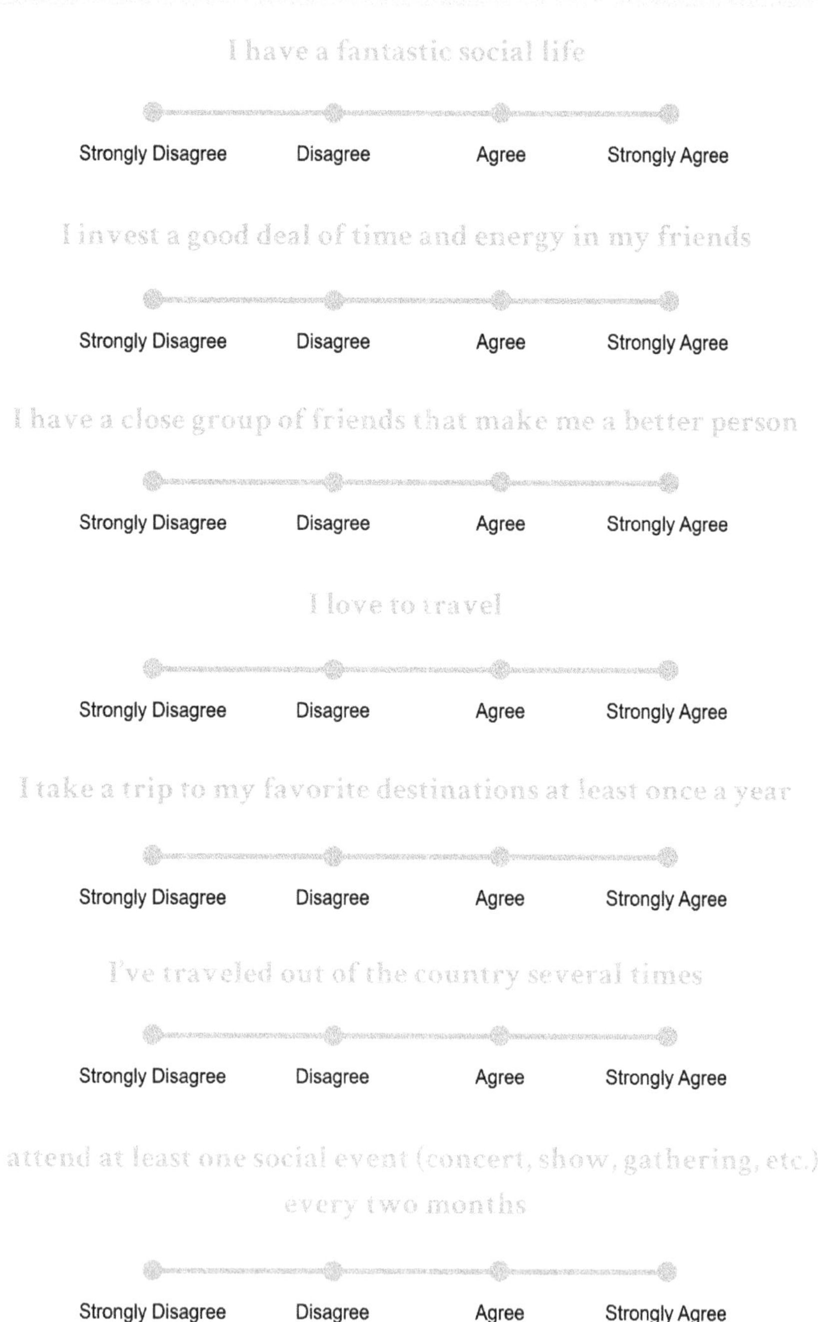

I pay close attention to the relationships that nourish me versus the relationships that drain me.

On a scale of 1 - 10, how would you rate your current Social Life & Travel?

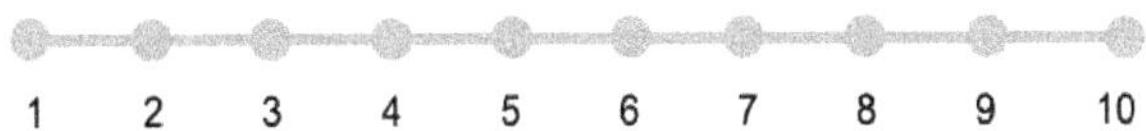


Based on your ratings, what are three actions you can immediately take to move towards a 10 rating in this category?

1. ................................................................................................................
................................................................................................................
................................................................................................................

2. ................................................................................................................
................................................................................................................
................................................................................................................

3. ................................................................................................................
................................................................................................................
................................................................................................................

# Leisure & Self-Care

I purchase something or do something for myself at least once a month

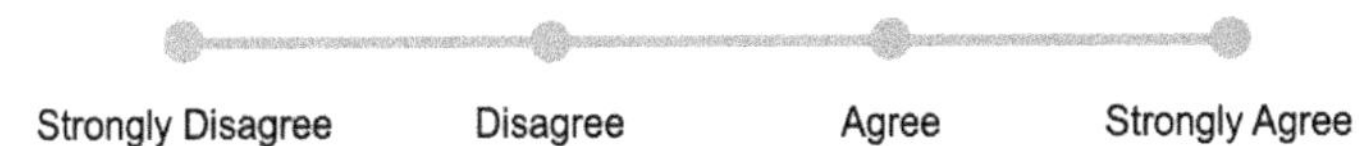


On a scale of 1 - 10, how would you rate your current Leisure & Self-Care?

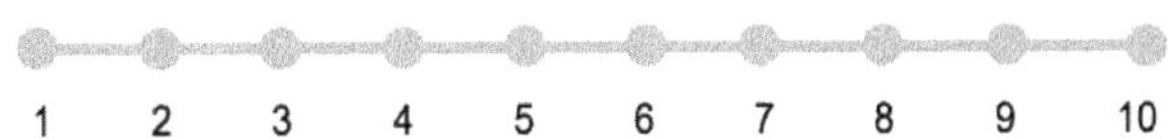


Based on your ratings, what are three actions you can immediately take to move towards a 10 rating in this category?

1. ..........................................................................................

..........................................................................................

..........................................................................................

2. ..........................................................................................

..........................................................................................

..........................................................................................

3. ..........................................................................................

..........................................................................................

..........................................................................................

# Business & Career

My career is fulfilling to me, and I love what I do

Strongly Disagree | Disagree | Agree | Strongly Agree

I wake up every morning looking forward to work

Strongly Disagree | Disagree | Agree | Strongly Agree

I'm very good at what I do

Strongly Disagree | Disagree | Agree | Strongly Agree

I constantly invest in improving my job skills

Strongly Disagree | Disagree | Agree | Strongly Agree

I could work at my current job/business for the rest of my life and be happy

Strongly Disagree | Disagree | Agree | Strongly Agree

My career/business keeps me learning and growing

Strongly Disagree | Disagree | Agree | Strongly Agree

I like the people that I work with

Strongly Disagree | Disagree | Agree | Strongly Agree

I feel like I'm paid fair wages for my job, or I charge enough in my business

Strongly Disagree Disagree Agree Strongly Agree

On a scale of 1 - 10, how would you rate your current Business & Career?

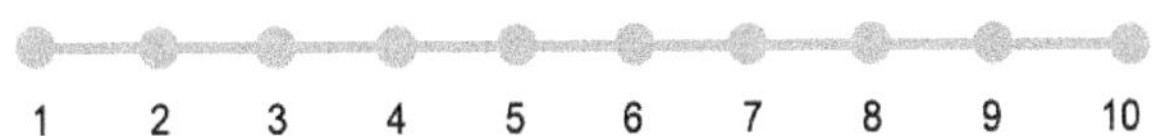


Based on your ratings, what are three actions you can immediately take to move towards a 10 rating in this category?

1. ..............................................................................................................
..............................................................................................................
..............................................................................................................
..............................................................................................................

2. ..............................................................................................................
..............................................................................................................
..............................................................................................................
..............................................................................................................

3. ..............................................................................................................
..............................................................................................................
..............................................................................................................
..............................................................................................................

# Money & Finances

My ideal income is .......................... a year

Strongly Disagree　　Disagree　　Agree　　Strongly Agree

On a scale of 1 - 10, how would you rate your current Money & Finances?

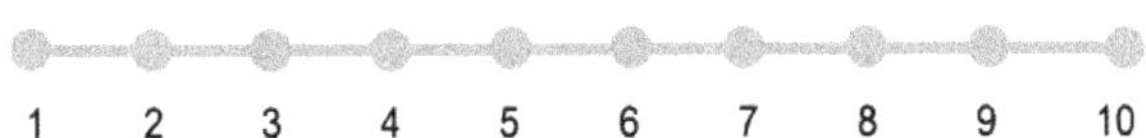


Based on your ratings, what are three actions you can immediately take to move towards a 10 rating in this category?

1. ..........................................................................................
..........................................................................................
..........................................................................................
..........................................................................................

2. ..........................................................................................
..........................................................................................
..........................................................................................
..........................................................................................

3. ..........................................................................................
..........................................................................................
..........................................................................................
..........................................................................................

# My Suitcase

For many people, these will be the most important exercises that empower you to actually make needed changes that have a lasting impact on your health and your life. We spend most of our lives grinding to add as many things as we can, with the hope that when we get those things, it will increase our happiness, value, and peace. But, soon, we learn the hard way that even as we attain and achieve things, it doesn't profoundly impact our lives as we expected.

Let me let you in on a bit of a secret that will save you so much time, energy, and disappointment. When you base your happiness, fulfillment, and peace on anything you need to add outside of yourself, you will never be satisfied. The bar will just keep moving. The more you get, the more you'll want.

You got that job, and it didn't fulfill you as you expected.

You have more money, and it still feels like it's not enough.

You found that relationship that you wanted and still feel like you have voids.

Here's the point. What you're looking for may not be a matter of adding something to your life but letting some things go. It's like adding with subtraction.

In this section, we will go through several powerful exercises that I refer to as your Suitcase.

Your suitcase symbolizes which things you choose to pack up and carry with you and which things you choose to unpack and leave behind.

You'll learn that there are things that you put in your suitcase that you have carried around for a long time. The more things you pack, the heavier it gets. Life is happening to all of us, so it's natural that you will accumulate many experiences, memories, and emotions over the years. The thing I want you to understand is that it's not as much about what you're carrying as it is about how what you're carrying is impacting how aligned you are with your life's deepest desires.

Certain things that you pack will be heavier than others. Heavier things include unexpressed and unresolved emotions, pain, trauma, unanswered questions, and a self-defeating mindset. Every time you pack one of those in your suitcase, it's like putting a 10-pound weight in your suitcase. Eventually, your suitcase becomes too heavy for you to carry. Then you have to drag your suitcase. Imagine the toll trying to carry a 300-pound suitcase will have on you physically, emotionally, and mentally. Now, think about dragging that same suitcase into every season of your life, every relationship, and every situation.

That's what many of us do our entire lives. Either we don't realize we're doing it or accept it as what we have to do to survive. Today that ends!

You're going to drag your suitcase out of the closet, blow off the dust, throw it on the bed, and open it up. You're going on a trip. This is your journey to a life of more peace, more happiness, more joy, more love, and more fulfillment. The only way you're going to take this trip is to unpack the things weighing you down and only pack the things you need.

I know it's not an easy task. Before, when I went on vacation, I used to pack 2 weeks of clothes for a weekend, just in case I needed it. Of course, I didn't use most of what I packed and just made transporting that luggage much more complicated than it needed to be. Now, I only pack what I know I'm going to need. If by some chance, I left something or needed a few extra things, I would purchase it on the trip. But that rarely happens.

As you work through the exercises in this section, think about your suitcase. Think about the weight of the thing you're packing and if it's worth taking with you. Once your suitcase is packed, it has to be checked before you can make the trip. Imagine that you're at the airport checking your bag, and you have to put it on the scale before you go to the gate. Just like at the airport, if your bag is too heavy, you're going to have to unpack some things and throw them away, or you're going to have to pay a lot more money to get your bag checked. That fee can get expensive!

If you're a person who feels like you need to carry the weight of others, tell people "yes" when you want to say "no," feel drained from having too many obligations, and have a hard time setting boundaries, this section is going to change your life forever.

# Unpacking My Bag

Now that you understand the importance of the contents of your suitcase, it's time to decide what you need to unpack to let go of all the things, pain, people, and feelings that are holding you back from who you're meant to become.

Letting go isn't easy. Especially when it comes to letting go of people and situations you've had in your life for a long time.

There may be some mistakes you've made that you need to forgive yourself or some people you need to forgive so that you can move on.

Past trauma from your childhood or pain caused by a loved one that you never fully let go of could be weighing on your spirit.

There's a lot to unpack here. No pun intended! Unpacking will be an uncomfortable exercise that will force you to face things that you've been ignoring and running from. It will push you to be honest with yourself about challenging situations. You'll be tempted to figure in other people's opinions, thoughts, and needs as you think through this. Remember, this is all about you, your wants, your needs, and your life.

*Tip: It's best to do this exercise when alone and away from distractions for at least 20 minutes. Try going outside or a relaxing area with soft music so that you can focus.*

**When it comes to MY happiness, my peace, my life of fulfillment, and my wellbeing, I have to unpack:**

1. ............................................................................................................
2. ............................................................................................................
3. ............................................................................................................
4. ............................................................................................................
5. ............................................................................................................
6. ............................................................................................................
7. ............................................................................................................
8. ............................................................................................................
9. ............................................................................................................
10. ............................................................................................................
11. ............................................................................................................
12. ............................................................................................................
13. ............................................................................................................
14. ............................................................................................................
15. ............................................................................................................
16. ............................................................................................................
17. ............................................................................................................
18. ............................................................................................................
19. ............................................................................................................

Congratulations! How do you feel? I know that wasn't easy but you had the courage to do it anyway. That says a great deal about who you are and how dedicated you are to making the difficult decisions needed to change your life.

You've decided what things you need to unpack, now it's time to decide what things you need to pack up to take with you. This part should be fun and exciting. I want you to think about the things and the people who add the kind of value to your life that are aligned with the best of you. When you feel powerful, inspired, energized, and motivated. Compared to the things that you needed to unpack, these things are *light.*

These things don't weigh you down or hold you back, but rather they add to you. They help you grow, they make you stronger, and they bring you joy.

You're about to travel to this island that you are going to create and cultivate, what would you need to pack that would give you the best chance to be the best that you can be?

List all of the things that you're going to pack and take with you.

**When it comes to being the happiest, most powerful, most loving, and most successful version of myself, I have to pack:**

1. ..................................................................................................
2. ..................................................................................................
3. ..................................................................................................
4. ..................................................................................................
5. ..................................................................................................
6. ..................................................................................................
7. ..................................................................................................
8. ..................................................................................................
9. ..................................................................................................
10. ..................................................................................................
11. ..................................................................................................
12. ..................................................................................................
13. ..................................................................................................
14. ..................................................................................................
15. ..................................................................................................
16. ..................................................................................................
17. ..................................................................................................
18. ..................................................................................................
19. ..................................................................................................

# The Power of "No"

*No* is a power word. It gives us a definite sense of self. Saying "No" is an ideal opportunity to rediscover your priorities and understanding who you are.

Until we learn to say "No," we continue to be overwhelmed with too much to do and not enough time. Have you noticed that it's usually essential things impacted by not saying "No," like quality time with self or family, our health, and our stress levels?

Whether you learn to say "No" more often or just know to say "Yes" on your terms, it's time to release yourself from the burden of pleasing others. Give yourself time and freedom to be, and do what matters to you. Let's get started!

**When is it OK to say "No"?**

**You ABSOLUTELY MUST Say "No":**

- When you're stressed or overwhelmed
- When you're already doing too much
- When you're tired or sick

And REMEMBER

**You always HAVE A RIGHT to Say "No":**

- When it's someone else's issue
- When you feel taken for granted
- When it's something you don't want to do
- When there's something you'd MUCH rather do
- When it takes away from your values and wishes
- When you deserve or need some time to yourself

1. **What in your life do YOU need to say "No" to?**

*Just write down whatever pops into your head below.*

..........................................................................................................

..........................................................................................................

2. **What currently stops me from saying "No" to these things?**

..........................................................................................................

..........................................................................................................

3. **My Beliefs about saying "No"**

..........................................................................................................

..........................................................................................................

Simply answer the questions below with WHATEVER comes to mind. Don't worry about making contradictory statements (this may even be part of the problem!). Just capture anything and everything that comes up for you.

People who say "Yes" are:

..........................................................................................................

People who DON'T say "Yes" are:

..........................................................................................................

People who DON'T say "Yes" are:

..........................................................................................................People who DON'T say "No" are:

..........................................................................................................

What I've noticed about myself from this exercise is:

..........................................................................................................

..........................................................................................................

*"There are only two words that will always lead you to success. Those words are yes and no. Undoubtedly, you've mastered saying yes. So start practicing saying no. Your goals depend on it!"* ~ ***Jack Canfield***

4. **Understanding The "Yes" Trap**

   - **WHY do you say "Yes" when you'd rather be saying No?**

- **How do you BENEFIT by saying "Yes"?**
- **Understanding this is essential to say "No" - and valuing your own goals, needs, and time.**

When I say "Yes" I feel

................................................................................................................

................................................................................................................

................................................................................................................

................................................................................................................

When I say "Yes" I want other people to think I am

................................................................................................................

................................................................................................................

................................................................................................................

................................................................................................................

*Examples: Maybe you want people to like you, think you're reliable, hard-working, helpful, or to make yourself indispensable?*

By saying "Yes", what am I saying "No" to in my own life?

................................................................................................................

................................................................................................................

................................................................................................................

................................................................................................................

*Whenever we say "Yes" to something, we're saying "No" to something else - even if that something is simply relaxing!*

When I say "No" I feel

................................................................................................................

................................................................................................................

................................................................................................................

When I say "No" I worry other people will think I am .

................................................................................................................

.....................................................................................................................

.....................................................................................................................

If I said "No", I could say "Yes" to these things in my life

.....................................................................................................................

.....................................................................................................................

.....................................................................................................................

What could you make room for that is truly important to you?

.....................................................................................................................

.....................................................................................................................

.....................................................................................................................

Lastly, when I say "Yes", but I really want to say "No" I feel

.....................................................................................................................

.....................................................................................................................

.....................................................................................................................

My biggest fears about saying "No" are

.....................................................................................................................

.....................................................................................................................

.....................................................................................................................

5. **The other "Know" - Know YOUR Priorities!**

    - **How can we say "No" assertively when we don't know WHY we're saying "No"?**
    - **To say "No" effectively, you need to be in touch with what's important to YOU - to know YOUR priorities in life.**
    - **Then it's much easier to say "No" because we're clear on what we want and need instead.**

What is MOST important to ME in life?

.....................................................................................................................

How would I like to spend MORE time?

..........................................................................................................

Where would I like to spend LESS time?

..........................................................................................................

What is my top priority this YEAR?

..........................................................................................................

What is my top priority this MONTH?

..........................................................................................................

What is my top priority this WEEK?

..........................................................................................................

If I had a MAGIC WAND I would .

..........................................................................................................

My Top 3 Priorities in life right now are:

1. ..........................................................................................................
2. ..........................................................................................................
3. ..........................................................................................................

How am I meeting my Top 3 Priorities in life right now?

..........................................................................................................

..........................................................................................................

..........................................................................................................

..........................................................................................................

**Some thoughts about saying no**

**Managing the Guilt:**

As you learn to say "No" more, you'll probably feel more guilt. This guilt is a sign that you're making meaningful, positive changes in your life.

**Evaluate EACH situation:**

As with most things in life, there is no one size fits all answer. Everything depends on the relative importance of the situation, people affected, what's going on in your life at the time, the person asking, your history with them, etc.

**Changing gradually is just fine:**

If you have been a "Yes" person in the past, you may want to become a person who says "No gradually." Take your time and practice on small things, working up to larger "No"s.

**Soften the blow:**

If you decide to go all out with your "No's," remember that others may find this a bit of a shock. It may help (although it's by no means necessary!) to find your way to soften it for them.

**Practicing:**

Try imagining you're already comfortable saying "No" and mentally rehearse difficult situations.

**Feeling good:**

When "No" is the correct answer for you, say it pleasantly, assertively, and with conviction. If it leaves you feeling strong and good in yourself (even if there is some guilt), then you've made the right choice for yourself!

**6. Preparing to Say "No."**

In what SPECIFIC areas or situations in my life do I need to be saying "No" more?

1. ..........................................................................................
   ..........................................................................................
   ..........................................................................................

2. ..........................................................................................
   ..........................................................................................
   ..........................................................................................

3. ..........................................................................................
   ..........................................................................................
   ..........................................................................................

**My NEW BELIEFS about Saying "No" are:**

1. ..........................................................................................
   ..........................................................................................
   ..........................................................................................
   ..........................................................................................
   ..........................................................................................

2. ..........................................................................................
   ..........................................................................................
   ..........................................................................................
   ..........................................................................................
   ..........................................................................................

3. ..........................................................................................
   ..........................................................................................
   ..........................................................................................
   ..........................................................................................
   ..........................................................................................

7. **My "Saying No" Plan!**

If you want things to be different, you will need to do things differently - but you can't change everything at once.

Using your answers to all the questions above and anything else you already know about yourself, identify three steps to get you started. Be as specific as you can!

**1st Action**

When..........................................................................................

asks ..........................................................................................

then I will ..................................................................................

**2nd Action**

When...............................................................................................

asks ...............................................................................................

then I will ......................................................................................

**3rd Action**

When...............................................................................................

asks ...............................................................................................

then I will ......................................................................................

*Now copy these out on post-it notes and stick them in your car, wallet, locker, fridge door, desk drawer, or any place where you will see them often.*

**8. Helpful Tips & Techniques for Saying "No."**

**Helpful Tips:**

**Tell the truth:**

ALWAYS find a way to be truthful. There's nothing worse than being caught in a lie. But you can leave out information (like that you could reschedule an appointment, so you are available) to protect your "No"...

**Timing can be everything:**

No does not mean "No forever." Sometimes you just need time or circumstances to be correct. So, don't pressure yourself into giving a response if you're not ready. Sometimes you just need time to figure out if it's a "No," a "Not now," or a "Never."

**Stay firm:**

People who are used to relying on you saying yes will try to persuade you. Don't get drawn into a discussion. Just repeat your No and have phrases ready. "I'm unavailable," "I can't right now," or "I have other commitments."

**Helpful Techniques:**

**SIMPLE**

1. A simple "No, but thanks for asking/thinking of me."

**SOMETHING ELSE**

2. A simple "I'm already doing ................. / have a dentist appointment"

**BUY YOURSELF TIME – when unsure how you feel or need time to prepare a response**

3. "I'm away from my desk right now. Can I let you know once I have my schedule in front of me?"
4. I'm just in the middle of something/a tight deadline. Can I get back to you tomorrow/next week?"

**DEFERRAL - good for other people's problems and issues**

5. "I'm crazy busy this week/month. Can it wait until next week/ month?"

**TRANSFER - good for maintaining relationships and still being helpful**

6. Suggest who else could do it, "I know James loves that kind of thing."
7. "I don't feel comfortable/have enough experience to help you with that, but Tiffany might be able to."

**RETURNING THE NO - good for those who take advantage of your good nature!**

8. "I can't do it right now - but I'd be glad to show you how to do it yourself."

**REQUESTING PRIORITY - good for dealing with your boss/when you're at work!**

9. Ask for the priority. "Which one do you think I need to focus on first?" OR "If I do this, what would you like me to stop working on?"

**PRIORITIZING YOURSELF - stay in control of your life and feel good about yourself!**

10. "I'd love to help, but I'm focusing on .................. (this report) right now."
11. OR "I don't have time for anything except ..................(this project/ my family) at the moment."

# Filling My Cup

Energy is everything! Understand the kind and quality of energy that you allow into your personal space is critical to your life of happiness and success. Some things continually drain your energy and keep you from being effective in the areas of your life that are most important.

This exercise is all about determining what things, people, or situations in your life are draining you. It's not just about feeling physically exhausted, and these things impact your emotional, spiritual, and mental health as well.

Think of the analogy of the cup, bucket, or vase. You are a vessel, physically and spiritually. If your cup is empty from being drained, you're not going to have anything left to pour out. Not having anything left to pour leads to feeling exhausted, overwhelmed, and empty. That leaves you with nothing left to give to the people you love, nothing left to give to your dreams, and nothing left to give to yourself.

Here's your chance to identify what things are emptying your cup, in essence, emptying you.

**List all of the top 10 things that are emptying your cup/bucket.** (If you have more than 10, you can write them on a separate page.)

*Examples: situations, relationships, bad habits, people, unmet needs, unresolved issues, a job, etc.*

1. ..........................................................................................................
   ..........................................................................................................

2. ..........................................................................................................
   ..........................................................................................................

3. ..........................................................................................................
   ..........................................................................................................

4. ..........................................................................................................
   ..........................................................................................................

5. ..........................................................................................................
   ..........................................................................................................

6. ..........................................................................................................
   ..........................................................................................................

7. ..........................................................................................................
   ..........................................................................................................

8. ..........................................................................................................
   ..........................................................................................................

9. ..........................................................................................................
   ..........................................................................................................

10. ..........................................................................................................
    ..........................................................................................................

Now that you've determined what things empty your cup/bucket, it's time to figure out what things are filling it. There's nothing like a situation that takes and takes but never gives anything back. There was probably a situation or person that came to mind as you read that last sentence.

**List the top 10 things that fill your cup/bucket.** (If you have more than 10, you can write them on a separate page.)

*These are going to be things and people who pour into you, fill you and energize you.*

1. ........................................................................................................
........................................................................................................

2. ........................................................................................................
........................................................................................................

3. ........................................................................................................
........................................................................................................

4. ........................................................................................................
........................................................................................................

5. ........................................................................................................
........................................................................................................

6. ........................................................................................................
........................................................................................................

7. ........................................................................................................
........................................................................................................

8. ........................................................................................................
........................................................................................................

9. ........................................................................................................
........................................................................................................

10. ........................................................................................................
........................................................................................................

# My NOT To-Do List

This exercise helps you STOP things that slow you down or get in the way of achieving your goals and being effective. You probably already have an idea of things you coils stop doing.

First, list what you would like to get out of this exercise. For example, you may want to be more focused, be less stressed, stick to a diet, get more done, etc.

..........................................................................................................................

..........................................................................................................................

..........................................................................................................................

..........................................................................................................................

..........................................................................................................................

..........................................................................................................................

..........................................................................................................................

..........................................................................................................................

The goal is to identify things NOT to do. These are usually activities where you get distracted or sabotage yourself. To stop doing something, we often need to take action by doing something else instead. The more specific you can be, the better. Areas many people struggle with are checking email, scrolling through social media, exercise habits, and goals that keep getting recycled year after year.

| Distraction | Impact | My NOT to-DO. I will STOP | I will instead: |
|---|---|---|---|
| | | | |

**Example #1**

**Distraction** (be specific so you are clear on how you distract yourself)

I want to be more focused. I keep stopping to check my email and I feel like I have to respond to them immediately.

**Impact** (be specific to get the true impact)

I lose focus for 15 minutes each time!

**My NOT to-DO. I will STOP:**

Answer each email as it arrives.

**I will instead:**

Check email at 9 AM, 12 PM, and 4 PM

**Example #2**

**Distraction**

I want to stick to my diet. I don't plan my meals or bring lunch, and I am so hungry and short on time that I need food fast

**Impact** (be specific to get the true impact)

I go get fast food and don't stick to my diet.

**My NOT to-DO. I will STOP:**

Putting off grocery shopping.

**I will instead:**

I grocery shop on Sundays and plan my meals for the week.

1. **Distraction** (be specific so you are clear on how you distract yourself)

.........................................................................................................................

**Impact** (be specific to get the true impact)

.........................................................................................................................

**My NOT to-DO. I will STOP:**

..........................................................................................................

**I will instead:**

..........................................................................................................

2. **Distraction** (be specific so you are clear on how you distract yourself)

..........................................................................................................

**Impact** (be specific to get the true impact)

..........................................................................................................

**My NOT to-DO. I will STOP:**

..........................................................................................................

**I will instead:**

..........................................................................................................

3. **Distraction** (be specific so you are clear on how you distract yourself)

..........................................................................................................

**Impact** (be specific to get the true impact)

..........................................................................................................

**My NOT to-DO. I will STOP:**

..........................................................................................................

**I will instead:**

..........................................................................................................

4. **Distraction** (be specific so you are clear on how you distract yourself)

..........................................................................................................

**Impact** (be specific to get the true impact)

..........................................................................................................

**My NOT to-DO. I will STOP:**

..........................................................................................................

**I will instead:**

..........................................................................................................

# My Reflections

# Reflections

.................................................................. ............... ......................

Name of Reflection Page Date

What message do you think the author wants you to take from this reflection?

........................................................................................................................

........................................................................................................................

What part of the reflection stood out to you the most? Why?

........................................................................................................................

........................................................................................................................

How did it make you feel? Why?

........................................................................................................................

........................................................................................................................

What important lessons or reminders can you take from this?

........................................................................................................................

........................................................................................................................

How can you put what you've learned into action to become who you're meant to be and feel more fulfilled in that area of your life?

........................................................................................................................

........................................................................................................................

What's the first action you promise to take within the next week?

........................................................................................................................

........................................................................................................................

*It doesn't have to be a big step. Even baby steps move you forward.*

# Reflections

........................................................................ ................ ........................

Name of Reflection Page Date

What message do you think the author wants you to take from this reflection?

........................................................................................................................................

........................................................................................................................................

What part of the reflection stood out to you the most? Why?

........................................................................................................................................

........................................................................................................................................

How did it make you feel? Why?

........................................................................................................................................

........................................................................................................................................

What important lessons or reminders can you take from this?

........................................................................................................................................

........................................................................................................................................

How can you put what you've learned into action to become who you're meant to be and feel more fulfilled in that area of your life?

........................................................................................................................................

........................................................................................................................................

What's the first action you promise to take within the next week?

........................................................................................................................................

........................................................................................................................................

*It doesn't have to be a big step. Even baby steps move you forward.*

# Reflections

........................................................................ ................ ........................

Name of Reflection Page Date

What message do you think the author wants you to take from this reflection?

..........................................................................................................................................

..........................................................................................................................................

What part of the reflection stood out to you the most? Why?

..........................................................................................................................................

..........................................................................................................................................

How did it make you feel? Why?

..........................................................................................................................................

..........................................................................................................................................

What important lessons or reminders can you take from this?

..........................................................................................................................................

..........................................................................................................................................

How can you put what you've learned into action to become who you're meant to be and feel more fulfilled in that area of your life?

..........................................................................................................................................

..........................................................................................................................................

What's the first action you promise to take within the next week?

..........................................................................................................................................

..........................................................................................................................................

*It doesn't have to be a big step. Even baby steps move you forward.*

# Reflections

........................................................................ ............... ......................

Name of Reflection Page Date

What message do you think the author wants you to take from this reflection?

..........................................................................................................................

..........................................................................................................................

What part of the reflection stood out to you the most? Why?

..........................................................................................................................

..........................................................................................................................

How did it make you feel? Why?

..........................................................................................................................

..........................................................................................................................

What important lessons or reminders can you take from this?

..........................................................................................................................

..........................................................................................................................

How can you put what you've learned into action to become who you're meant to be and feel more fulfilled in that area of your life?

..........................................................................................................................

..........................................................................................................................

What's the first action you promise to take within the next week?

..........................................................................................................................

..........................................................................................................................

*It doesn't have to be a big step. Even baby steps move you forward.*

# Reflections

........................................................................ ................ ........................

Name of Reflection Page Date

What message do you think the author wants you to take from this reflection?

..................................................................................................................................

..................................................................................................................................

What part of the reflection stood out to you the most? Why?

..................................................................................................................................

..................................................................................................................................

How did it make you feel? Why?

..................................................................................................................................

..................................................................................................................................

What important lessons or reminders can you take from this?

..................................................................................................................................

..................................................................................................................................

How can you put what you've learned into action to become who you're meant to be and feel more fulfilled in that area of your life?

..................................................................................................................................

..................................................................................................................................

What's the first action you promise to take within the next week?

..................................................................................................................................

..................................................................................................................................

*It doesn't have to be a big step. Even baby steps move you forward.*

# Reflections

.................................................................... ............... .....................

Name of Reflection Page Date

What message do you think the author wants you to take from this reflection?

.............................................................................................................................

.............................................................................................................................

What part of the reflection stood out to you the most? Why?

.............................................................................................................................

.............................................................................................................................

How did it make you feel? Why?

.............................................................................................................................

.............................................................................................................................

What important lessons or reminders can you take from this?

.............................................................................................................................

.............................................................................................................................

How can you put what you've learned into action to become who you're meant to be and feel more fulfilled in that area of your life?

.............................................................................................................................

.............................................................................................................................

What's the first action you promise to take within the next week?

.............................................................................................................................

.............................................................................................................................

*It doesn't have to be a big step. Even baby steps move you forward.*

# Reflections

........................................................................ ............... .......................

Name of Reflection Page Date

What message do you think the author wants you to take from this reflection?

..................................................................................................................................

..................................................................................................................................

What part of the reflection stood out to you the most? Why?

..................................................................................................................................

..................................................................................................................................

How did it make you feel? Why?

..................................................................................................................................

..................................................................................................................................

What important lessons or reminders can you take from this?

..................................................................................................................................

..................................................................................................................................

How can you put what you've learned into action to become who you're meant to be and feel more fulfilled in that area of your life?

..................................................................................................................................

..................................................................................................................................

What's the first action you promise to take within the next week?

..................................................................................................................................

..................................................................................................................................

*It doesn't have to be a big step. Even baby steps move you forward.*

# Reflections

.................................................................... ................ ......................

Name of Reflection Page Date

What message do you think the author wants you to take from this reflection?

..............................................................................................................................

..............................................................................................................................

What part of the reflection stood out to you the most? Why?

..............................................................................................................................

..............................................................................................................................

How did it make you feel? Why?

..............................................................................................................................

..............................................................................................................................

What important lessons or reminders can you take from this?

..............................................................................................................................

..............................................................................................................................

How can you put what you've learned into action to become who you're meant to be and feel more fulfilled in that area of your life?

..............................................................................................................................

..............................................................................................................................

What's the first action you promise to take within the next week?

..............................................................................................................................

..............................................................................................................................

*It doesn't have to be a big step. Even baby steps move you forward.*

# Reflections

.............................................................. ................ ......................

Name of Reflection Page Date

What message do you think the author wants you to take from this reflection?

..............................................................................................................

..............................................................................................................

What part of the reflection stood out to you the most? Why?

..............................................................................................................

..............................................................................................................

How did it make you feel? Why?

..............................................................................................................

..............................................................................................................

What important lessons or reminders can you take from this?

..............................................................................................................

..............................................................................................................

How can you put what you've learned into action to become who you're meant to be and feel more fulfilled in that area of your life?

..............................................................................................................

..............................................................................................................

What's the first action you promise to take within the next week?

..............................................................................................................

..............................................................................................................

*It doesn't have to be a big step. Even baby steps move you forward.*

# Reflections

........................................................................ ................ ........................

Name of Reflection Page Date

What message do you think the author wants you to take from this reflection?

........................................................................................................................................

........................................................................................................................................

What part of the reflection stood out to you the most? Why?

........................................................................................................................................

........................................................................................................................................

How did it make you feel? Why?

........................................................................................................................................

........................................................................................................................................

What important lessons or reminders can you take from this?

........................................................................................................................................

........................................................................................................................................

How can you put what you've learned into action to become who you're meant to be and feel more fulfilled in that area of your life?

........................................................................................................................................

........................................................................................................................................

What's the first action you promise to take within the next week?

........................................................................................................................................

........................................................................................................................................

*It doesn't have to be a big step. Even baby steps move you forward.*

# Reflections

..................................................................... ............... ......................

Name of Reflection Page Date

What message do you think the author wants you to take from this reflection?

..........................................................................................................................

..........................................................................................................................

What part of the reflection stood out to you the most? Why?

..........................................................................................................................

..........................................................................................................................

How did it make you feel? Why?

..........................................................................................................................

..........................................................................................................................

What important lessons or reminders can you take from this?

..........................................................................................................................

..........................................................................................................................

How can you put what you've learned into action to become who you're meant to be and feel more fulfilled in that area of your life?

..........................................................................................................................

..........................................................................................................................

What's the first action you promise to take within the next week?

..........................................................................................................................

..........................................................................................................................

*It doesn't have to be a big step. Even baby steps move you forward.*

# Reflections

........................................................................ ................ ........................

Name of Reflection Page Date

What message do you think the author wants you to take from this reflection?

..............................................................................................................................

..............................................................................................................................

What part of the reflection stood out to you the most? Why?

..............................................................................................................................

..............................................................................................................................

How did it make you feel? Why?

..............................................................................................................................

..............................................................................................................................

What important lessons or reminders can you take from this?

..............................................................................................................................

..............................................................................................................................

How can you put what you've learned into action to become who you're meant to be and feel more fulfilled in that area of your life?

..............................................................................................................................

..............................................................................................................................

What's the first action you promise to take within the next week?

..............................................................................................................................

..............................................................................................................................

*It doesn't have to be a big step. Even baby steps move you forward.*

# Reflections

.............................................................. ................ ......................

Name of Reflection Page Date

What message do you think the author wants you to take from this reflection?

..........................................................................................................

..........................................................................................................

What part of the reflection stood out to you the most? Why?

..........................................................................................................

..........................................................................................................

How did it make you feel? Why?

..........................................................................................................

..........................................................................................................

What important lessons or reminders can you take from this?

..........................................................................................................

..........................................................................................................

How can you put what you've learned into action to become who you're meant to be and feel more fulfilled in that area of your life?

..........................................................................................................

..........................................................................................................

What's the first action you promise to take within the next week?

..........................................................................................................

..........................................................................................................

*It doesn't have to be a big step. Even baby steps move you forward.*

# Reflections

.............................................................. ............... ......................

Name of Reflection Page Date

What message do you think the author wants you to take from this reflection?

..........................................................................................................................

..........................................................................................................................

What part of the reflection stood out to you the most? Why?

..........................................................................................................................

..........................................................................................................................

How did it make you feel? Why?

..........................................................................................................................

..........................................................................................................................

What important lessons or reminders can you take from this?

..........................................................................................................................

..........................................................................................................................

How can you put what you've learned into action to become who you're meant to be and feel more fulfilled in that area of your life?

..........................................................................................................................

..........................................................................................................................

What's the first action you promise to take within the next week?

..........................................................................................................................

..........................................................................................................................

*It doesn't have to be a big step. Even baby steps move you forward.*

# Reflections

.................................................................. ............... ......................

Name of Reflection Page Date

What message do you think the author wants you to take from this reflection?

..............................................................................................................................

..............................................................................................................................

What part of the reflection stood out to you the most? Why?

..............................................................................................................................

..............................................................................................................................

How did it make you feel? Why?

..............................................................................................................................

..............................................................................................................................

What important lessons or reminders can you take from this?

..............................................................................................................................

..............................................................................................................................

How can you put what you've learned into action to become who you're meant to be and feel more fulfilled in that area of your life?

..............................................................................................................................

..............................................................................................................................

What's the first action you promise to take within the next week?

..............................................................................................................................

..............................................................................................................................

*It doesn't have to be a big step. Even baby steps move you forward.*

# Reflections

.................................................................... ................ ........................

Name of Reflection Page Date

What message do you think the author wants you to take from this reflection?

..............................................................................................................................

..............................................................................................................................

What part of the reflection stood out to you the most? Why?

..............................................................................................................................

..............................................................................................................................

How did it make you feel? Why?

..............................................................................................................................

..............................................................................................................................

What important lessons or reminders can you take from this?

..............................................................................................................................

..............................................................................................................................

How can you put what you've learned into action to become who you're meant to be and feel more fulfilled in that area of your life?

..............................................................................................................................

..............................................................................................................................

What's the first action you promise to take within the next week?

..............................................................................................................................

..............................................................................................................................

*It doesn't have to be a big step. Even baby steps move you forward.*

# Reflections

........................................................................ ................ ........................

Name of Reflection Page Date

What message do you think the author wants you to take from this reflection?

..............................................................................................................................

..............................................................................................................................

What part of the reflection stood out to you the most? Why?

..............................................................................................................................

..............................................................................................................................

How did it make you feel? Why?

..............................................................................................................................

..............................................................................................................................

What important lessons or reminders can you take from this?

..............................................................................................................................

..............................................................................................................................

How can you put what you've learned into action to become who you're meant to be and feel more fulfilled in that area of your life?

..............................................................................................................................

..............................................................................................................................

What's the first action you promise to take within the next week?

..............................................................................................................................

..............................................................................................................................

*It doesn't have to be a big step. Even baby steps move you forward.*

# Reflections

.................................................................. ............... ......................

Name of Reflection Page Date

What message do you think the author wants you to take from this reflection?

........................................................................................................................

........................................................................................................................

What part of the reflection stood out to you the most? Why?

........................................................................................................................

........................................................................................................................

How did it make you feel? Why?

........................................................................................................................

........................................................................................................................

What important lessons or reminders can you take from this?

........................................................................................................................

........................................................................................................................

How can you put what you've learned into action to become who you're meant to be and feel more fulfilled in that area of your life?

........................................................................................................................

........................................................................................................................

What's the first action you promise to take within the next week?

........................................................................................................................

........................................................................................................................

*It doesn't have to be a big step. Even baby steps move you forward.*

# Reflections

.............................................................. ............... ......................

Name of Reflection Page Date

What message do you think the author wants you to take from this reflection?

...................................................................................................................

...................................................................................................................

What part of the reflection stood out to you the most? Why?

...................................................................................................................

...................................................................................................................

How did it make you feel? Why?

...................................................................................................................

...................................................................................................................

What important lessons or reminders can you take from this?

...................................................................................................................

...................................................................................................................

How can you put what you've learned into action to become who you're meant to be and feel more fulfilled in that area of your life?

...................................................................................................................

...................................................................................................................

What's the first action you promise to take within the next week?

...................................................................................................................

...................................................................................................................

*It doesn't have to be a big step. Even baby steps move you forward.*

# Reflections

........................................................................ ................ .......................

Name of Reflection Page Date

What message do you think the author wants you to take from this reflection?

........................................................................................................................................

........................................................................................................................................

What part of the reflection stood out to you the most? Why?

........................................................................................................................................

........................................................................................................................................

How did it make you feel? Why?

........................................................................................................................................

........................................................................................................................................

What important lessons or reminders can you take from this?

........................................................................................................................................

........................................................................................................................................

How can you put what you've learned into action to become who you're meant to be and feel more fulfilled in that area of your life?

........................................................................................................................................

........................................................................................................................................

What's the first action you promise to take within the next week?

........................................................................................................................................

........................................................................................................................................

*It doesn't have to be a big step. Even baby steps move you forward.*

# Reflections

........................................................................ ............... .......................

Name of Reflection Page Date

What message do you think the author wants you to take from this reflection?

..............................................................................................................................

..............................................................................................................................

What part of the reflection stood out to you the most? Why?

..............................................................................................................................

..............................................................................................................................

How did it make you feel? Why?

..............................................................................................................................

..............................................................................................................................

What important lessons or reminders can you take from this?

..............................................................................................................................

..............................................................................................................................

How can you put what you've learned into action to become who you're meant to be and feel more fulfilled in that area of your life?

..............................................................................................................................

..............................................................................................................................

What's the first action you promise to take within the next week?

..............................................................................................................................

..............................................................................................................................

*It doesn't have to be a big step. Even baby steps move you forward.*

# Reflections

.................................................................. ............... ......................

Name of Reflection Page Date

What message do you think the author wants you to take from this reflection?

..........................................................................................................................

..........................................................................................................................

What part of the reflection stood out to you the most? Why?

..........................................................................................................................

..........................................................................................................................

How did it make you feel? Why?

..........................................................................................................................

..........................................................................................................................

What important lessons or reminders can you take from this?

..........................................................................................................................

..........................................................................................................................

How can you put what you've learned into action to become who you're meant to be and feel more fulfilled in that area of your life?

..........................................................................................................................

..........................................................................................................................

What's the first action you promise to take within the next week?

..........................................................................................................................

..........................................................................................................................

*It doesn't have to be a big step. Even baby steps move you forward.*

# Reflections

.................................................................... ............... ......................

Name of Reflection Page Date

What message do you think the author wants you to take from this reflection?

..........................................................................................................................

..........................................................................................................................

What part of the reflection stood out to you the most? Why?

..........................................................................................................................

..........................................................................................................................

How did it make you feel? Why?

..........................................................................................................................

..........................................................................................................................

What important lessons or reminders can you take from this?

..........................................................................................................................

..........................................................................................................................

How can you put what you've learned into action to become who you're meant to be and feel more fulfilled in that area of your life?

..........................................................................................................................

..........................................................................................................................

What's the first action you promise to take within the next week?

..........................................................................................................................

..........................................................................................................................

*It doesn't have to be a big step. Even baby steps move you forward.*

# Reflections

.................................................................... ............... ......................

Name of Reflection Page Date

What message do you think the author wants you to take from this reflection?

..........................................................................................................................

..........................................................................................................................

What part of the reflection stood out to you the most? Why?

..........................................................................................................................

..........................................................................................................................

How did it make you feel? Why?

..........................................................................................................................

..........................................................................................................................

What important lessons or reminders can you take from this?

..........................................................................................................................

..........................................................................................................................

How can you put what you've learned into action to become who you're meant to be and feel more fulfilled in that area of your life?

..........................................................................................................................

..........................................................................................................................

What's the first action you promise to take within the next week?

..........................................................................................................................

..........................................................................................................................

*It doesn't have to be a big step. Even baby steps move you forward.*

# Reflections

........................................................................ ................ ........................

Name of Reflection | Page | Date

What message do you think the author wants you to take from this reflection?

.......................................................................................................................................

.......................................................................................................................................

What part of the reflection stood out to you the most? Why?

.......................................................................................................................................

.......................................................................................................................................

How did it make you feel? Why?

.......................................................................................................................................

.......................................................................................................................................

What important lessons or reminders can you take from this?

.......................................................................................................................................

.......................................................................................................................................

How can you put what you've learned into action to become who you're meant to be and feel more fulfilled in that area of your life?

.......................................................................................................................................

.......................................................................................................................................

What's the first action you promise to take within the next week?

.......................................................................................................................................

.......................................................................................................................................

*It doesn't have to be a big step. Even baby steps move you forward.*

# Reflections

Name of Reflection Page Date

What message do you think the author wants you to take from this reflection?

What part of the reflection stood out to you the most? Why?

How did it make you feel? Why?

What important lessons or reminders can you take from this?

How can you put what you've learned into action to become who you're meant to be and feel more fulfilled in that area of your life?

What's the first action you promise to take within the next week?

*It doesn't have to be a big step. Even baby steps move you forward.*

# Reflections

.................................................................... ............... ......................

Name of Reflection Page Date

What message do you think the author wants you to take from this reflection?

..........................................................................................................................

..........................................................................................................................

What part of the reflection stood out to you the most? Why?

..........................................................................................................................

..........................................................................................................................

How did it make you feel? Why?

..........................................................................................................................

..........................................................................................................................

What important lessons or reminders can you take from this?

..........................................................................................................................

..........................................................................................................................

How can you put what you've learned into action to become who you're meant to be and feel more fulfilled in that area of your life?

..........................................................................................................................

..........................................................................................................................

What's the first action you promise to take within the next week?

..........................................................................................................................

..........................................................................................................................

*It doesn't have to be a big step. Even baby steps move you forward.*

# Reflections

.................................................................. ................ ......................

Name of Reflection | Page | Date

What message do you think the author wants you to take from this reflection?

..........................................................................................................................

..........................................................................................................................

What part of the reflection stood out to you the most? Why?

..........................................................................................................................

..........................................................................................................................

How did it make you feel? Why?

..........................................................................................................................

..........................................................................................................................

What important lessons or reminders can you take from this?

..........................................................................................................................

..........................................................................................................................

How can you put what you've learned into action to become who you're meant to be and feel more fulfilled in that area of your life?

..........................................................................................................................

..........................................................................................................................

What's the first action you promise to take within the next week?

..........................................................................................................................

..........................................................................................................................

*It doesn't have to be a big step. Even baby steps move you forward.*

# Reflections

.................................................................. ............... ......................

Name of Reflection Page Date

What message do you think the author wants you to take from this reflection?

........................................................................................................................

........................................................................................................................

What part of the reflection stood out to you the most? Why?

........................................................................................................................

........................................................................................................................

How did it make you feel? Why?

........................................................................................................................

........................................................................................................................

What important lessons or reminders can you take from this?

........................................................................................................................

........................................................................................................................

How can you put what you've learned into action to become who you're meant to be and feel more fulfilled in that area of your life?

........................................................................................................................

........................................................................................................................

What's the first action you promise to take within the next week?

........................................................................................................................

........................................................................................................................

*It doesn't have to be a big step. Even baby steps move you forward.*

# Reflections

.................................................................. ............... ......................

Name of Reflection Page Date

What message do you think the author wants you to take from this reflection?

........................................................................................................................

........................................................................................................................

What part of the reflection stood out to you the most? Why?

........................................................................................................................

........................................................................................................................

How did it make you feel? Why?

........................................................................................................................

........................................................................................................................

What important lessons or reminders can you take from this?

........................................................................................................................

........................................................................................................................

How can you put what you've learned into action to become who you're meant to be and feel more fulfilled in that area of your life?

........................................................................................................................

........................................................................................................................

What's the first action you promise to take within the next week?

........................................................................................................................

........................................................................................................................

*It doesn't have to be a big step. Even baby steps move you forward.*

# My Intentions

# Morning

Date.......................................

I am grateful for:

.............................................................................................................

.............................................................................................................

.............................................................................................................

I'm looking forward to:

.............................................................................................................

.............................................................................................................

.............................................................................................................

Daily Intention or affirmation:

.............................................................................................................

.............................................................................................................

.............................................................................................................

# Evening

Good things that happened today

1. .......................................................................................................
.......................................................................................................
2. .......................................................................................................
.......................................................................................................
3. .......................................................................................................
.......................................................................................................

Things I can do to make tomorrow better

1. .......................................................................................................
.......................................................................................................
2. .......................................................................................................
.......................................................................................................
3. .......................................................................................................
.......................................................................................................

I showed myself love today by:

.............................................................................................................

.............................................................................................................

# Self-Check In

Date......................................

How do I feel right now?

..........................................................................................................

..........................................................................................................

..........................................................................................................

..........................................................................................................

..........................................................................................................

Why do I feel this way?

..........................................................................................................

..........................................................................................................

..........................................................................................................

..........................................................................................................

..........................................................................................................

If the feeling is a positive one, what's one action I can take to enhance it or repeat it?

..........................................................................................................

..........................................................................................................

..........................................................................................................

..........................................................................................................

..........................................................................................................

If the feeling is a negative one, what's one action I can take to improve my state, the situation, or raise my vibration?

..........................................................................................................

..........................................................................................................

..........................................................................................................

..........................................................................................................

..........................................................................................................

# Morning

Date......................................

I am grateful for:

..........................................................................................................

..........................................................................................................

..........................................................................................................

I'm looking forward to:

..........................................................................................................

..........................................................................................................

..........................................................................................................

Daily Intention or affirmation:

..........................................................................................................

..........................................................................................................

..........................................................................................................

# Evening

Good things that happened today

1. ..................................................................................................
   ..................................................................................................
2. ..................................................................................................
   ..................................................................................................
3. ..................................................................................................
   ..................................................................................................

Things I can do to make tomorrow better

1. ..................................................................................................
   ..................................................................................................
2. ..................................................................................................
   ..................................................................................................
3. ..................................................................................................
   ..................................................................................................

I showed myself love today by:

..........................................................................................................

..........................................................................................................

# Self-Check In

Date....................................

How do I feel right now?

..........................................................................................................
..........................................................................................................
..........................................................................................................
..........................................................................................................
..........................................................................................................

Why do I feel this way?

..........................................................................................................
..........................................................................................................
..........................................................................................................
..........................................................................................................
..........................................................................................................

If the feeling is a positive one, what's one action I can take to enhance it or repeat it?

..........................................................................................................
..........................................................................................................
..........................................................................................................
..........................................................................................................
..........................................................................................................

If the feeling is a negative one, what's one action I can take to improve my state, the situation, or raise my vibration?

..........................................................................................................
..........................................................................................................
..........................................................................................................
..........................................................................................................
..........................................................................................................

# Morning

Date.......................................

I am grateful for:

..............................................................................................................

..............................................................................................................

..............................................................................................................

I'm looking forward to:

..............................................................................................................

..............................................................................................................

..............................................................................................................

Daily Intention or affirmation:

..............................................................................................................

..............................................................................................................

..............................................................................................................

# Evening

Good things that happened today

1. .........................................................................................................
   .........................................................................................................
2. .........................................................................................................
   .........................................................................................................
3. .........................................................................................................
   .........................................................................................................

Things I can do to make tomorrow better

1. .........................................................................................................
   .........................................................................................................
2. .........................................................................................................
   .........................................................................................................
3. .........................................................................................................
   .........................................................................................................

I showed myself love today by:

..............................................................................................................

..............................................................................................................

# Self-Check In

Date......................................

How do I feel right now?

..........................................................................................................
..........................................................................................................
..........................................................................................................
..........................................................................................................
..........................................................................................................

Why do I feel this way?

..........................................................................................................
..........................................................................................................
..........................................................................................................
..........................................................................................................
..........................................................................................................

If the feeling is a positive one, what's one action I can take to enhance it or repeat it?

..........................................................................................................
..........................................................................................................
..........................................................................................................
..........................................................................................................
..........................................................................................................

If the feeling is a negative one, what's one action I can take to improve my state, the situation, or raise my vibration?

..........................................................................................................
..........................................................................................................
..........................................................................................................
..........................................................................................................
..........................................................................................................

# Morning

Date.......................................

I am grateful for:

..........................................................................................................................
..........................................................................................................................
..........................................................................................................................

I'm looking forward to:

..........................................................................................................................
..........................................................................................................................
..........................................................................................................................

Daily Intention or affirmation:

..........................................................................................................................
..........................................................................................................................
..........................................................................................................................

# Evening

Good things that happened today

1. ..................................................................................................................
   ..................................................................................................................
2. ..................................................................................................................
   ..................................................................................................................
3. ..................................................................................................................
   ..................................................................................................................

Things I can do to make tomorrow better

1. ..................................................................................................................
   ..................................................................................................................
2. ..................................................................................................................
   ..................................................................................................................
3. ..................................................................................................................
   ..................................................................................................................

I showed myself love today by:

..........................................................................................................................
..........................................................................................................................

# Self-Check In

Date.......................................

How do I feel right now?

..........................................................................................................

..........................................................................................................

..........................................................................................................

..........................................................................................................

..........................................................................................................

Why do I feel this way?

..........................................................................................................

..........................................................................................................

..........................................................................................................

..........................................................................................................

..........................................................................................................

If the feeling is a positive one, what's one action I can take to enhance it or repeat it?

..........................................................................................................

..........................................................................................................

..........................................................................................................

..........................................................................................................

..........................................................................................................

If the feeling is a negative one, what's one action I can take to improve my state, the situation, or raise my vibration?

..........................................................................................................

..........................................................................................................

..........................................................................................................

..........................................................................................................

..........................................................................................................

# Morning

Date......................................

I am grateful for:

..........................................................................................

..........................................................................................

..........................................................................................

I'm looking forward to:

..........................................................................................

..........................................................................................

..........................................................................................

Daily Intention or affirmation:

..........................................................................................

..........................................................................................

..........................................................................................

# Evening

Good things that happened today

1. ..........................................................................................
   ..........................................................................................
2. ..........................................................................................
   ..........................................................................................
3. ..........................................................................................
   ..........................................................................................

Things I can do to make tomorrow better

1. ..........................................................................................
   ..........................................................................................
2. ..........................................................................................
   ..........................................................................................
3. ..........................................................................................
   ..........................................................................................

I showed myself love today by:

..........................................................................................

..........................................................................................

# Self-Check In

Date........................................

How do I feel right now?

..................................................................................................

..................................................................................................

..................................................................................................

..................................................................................................

..................................................................................................

Why do I feel this way?

..................................................................................................

..................................................................................................

..................................................................................................

..................................................................................................

..................................................................................................

If the feeling is a positive one, what's one action I can take to enhance it or repeat it?

..................................................................................................

..................................................................................................

..................................................................................................

..................................................................................................

..................................................................................................

If the feeling is a negative one, what's one action I can take to improve my state, the situation, or raise my vibration?

..................................................................................................

..................................................................................................

..................................................................................................

..................................................................................................

..................................................................................................

# Morning

Date........................................

I am grateful for:

..........................................................................................................
..........................................................................................................
..........................................................................................................

I'm looking forward to:

..........................................................................................................
..........................................................................................................
..........................................................................................................

Daily Intention or affirmation:

..........................................................................................................
..........................................................................................................
..........................................................................................................

# Evening

Good things that happened today

1. ..................................................................................................
   ..................................................................................................
2. ..................................................................................................
   ..................................................................................................
3. ..................................................................................................
   ..................................................................................................

Things I can do to make tomorrow better

1. ..................................................................................................
   ..................................................................................................
2. ..................................................................................................
   ..................................................................................................
3. ..................................................................................................
   ..................................................................................................

I showed myself love today by:

..........................................................................................................
..........................................................................................................

# Self-Check In

Date.......................................

How do I feel right now?

..........................................................................................................

..........................................................................................................

..........................................................................................................

..........................................................................................................

..........................................................................................................

Why do I feel this way?

..........................................................................................................

..........................................................................................................

..........................................................................................................

..........................................................................................................

..........................................................................................................

If the feeling is a positive one, what's one action I can take to enhance it or repeat it?

..........................................................................................................

..........................................................................................................

..........................................................................................................

..........................................................................................................

..........................................................................................................

If the feeling is a negative one, what's one action I can take to improve my state, the situation, or raise my vibration?

..........................................................................................................

..........................................................................................................

..........................................................................................................

..........................................................................................................

..........................................................................................................

# Morning

Date........................................

I am grateful for:

.................................................................................................................
.................................................................................................................
.................................................................................................................

I'm looking forward to:

.................................................................................................................
.................................................................................................................
.................................................................................................................

Daily Intention or affirmation:

.................................................................................................................
.................................................................................................................
.................................................................................................................

# Evening

Good things that happened today

1. .........................................................................................................
   .........................................................................................................
2. .........................................................................................................
   .........................................................................................................
3. .........................................................................................................
   .........................................................................................................

Things I can do to make tomorrow better

1. .........................................................................................................
   .........................................................................................................
2. .........................................................................................................
   .........................................................................................................
3. .........................................................................................................
   .........................................................................................................

I showed myself love today by:

.................................................................................................................
.................................................................................................................

# Self-Check In

Date........................................

How do I feel right now?

.................................................................................................................

.................................................................................................................

.................................................................................................................

.................................................................................................................

.................................................................................................................

Why do I feel this way?

.................................................................................................................

.................................................................................................................

.................................................................................................................

.................................................................................................................

.................................................................................................................

If the feeling is a positive one, what's one action I can take to enhance it or repeat it?

.................................................................................................................

.................................................................................................................

.................................................................................................................

.................................................................................................................

.................................................................................................................

If the feeling is a negative one, what's one action I can take to improve my state, the situation, or raise my vibration?

.................................................................................................................

.................................................................................................................

.................................................................................................................

.................................................................................................................

.................................................................................................................

# Morning

Date.......................................

I am grateful for:

..........................................................................................

..........................................................................................

..........................................................................................

I'm looking forward to:

..........................................................................................

..........................................................................................

..........................................................................................

Daily Intention or affirmation:

..........................................................................................

..........................................................................................

..........................................................................................

# Evening

Good things that happened today

1. ....................................................................................
   ....................................................................................
2. ....................................................................................
   ....................................................................................
3. ....................................................................................
   ....................................................................................

Things I can do to make tomorrow better

1. ....................................................................................
   ....................................................................................
2. ....................................................................................
   ....................................................................................
3. ....................................................................................
   ....................................................................................

I showed myself love today by:

..........................................................................................

..........................................................................................

# Self-Check In

Date........................................

How do I feel right now?

.................................................................................................................

.................................................................................................................

.................................................................................................................

.................................................................................................................

.................................................................................................................

Why do I feel this way?

.................................................................................................................

.................................................................................................................

.................................................................................................................

.................................................................................................................

.................................................................................................................

If the feeling is a positive one, what's one action I can take to enhance it or repeat it?

.................................................................................................................

.................................................................................................................

.................................................................................................................

.................................................................................................................

.................................................................................................................

If the feeling is a negative one, what's one action I can take to improve my state, the situation, or raise my vibration?

.................................................................................................................

.................................................................................................................

.................................................................................................................

.................................................................................................................

.................................................................................................................

# Morning

Date.......................................

I am grateful for:

.....................................................................................................................

.....................................................................................................................

.....................................................................................................................

I'm looking forward to:

.....................................................................................................................

.....................................................................................................................

.....................................................................................................................

Daily Intention or affirmation:

.....................................................................................................................

.....................................................................................................................

.....................................................................................................................

# Evening

Good things that happened today

1. ..............................................................................................................
   ..............................................................................................................
2. ..............................................................................................................
   ..............................................................................................................
3. ..............................................................................................................
   ..............................................................................................................

Things I can do to make tomorrow better

1. ..............................................................................................................
   ..............................................................................................................
2. ..............................................................................................................
   ..............................................................................................................
3. ..............................................................................................................
   ..............................................................................................................

I showed myself love today by:

.....................................................................................................................

.....................................................................................................................

# Self-Check In

Date........................................

How do I feel right now?

..........................................................................................................

..........................................................................................................

..........................................................................................................

..........................................................................................................

..........................................................................................................

Why do I feel this way?

..........................................................................................................

..........................................................................................................

..........................................................................................................

..........................................................................................................

..........................................................................................................

If the feeling is a positive one, what's one action I can take to enhance it or repeat it?

..........................................................................................................

..........................................................................................................

..........................................................................................................

..........................................................................................................

..........................................................................................................

If the feeling is a negative one, what's one action I can take to improve my state, the situation, or raise my vibration?

..........................................................................................................

..........................................................................................................

..........................................................................................................

..........................................................................................................

..........................................................................................................

# Morning

Date....................................

I am grateful for:

..........................................................................................................

..........................................................................................................

..........................................................................................................

I'm looking forward to:

..........................................................................................................

..........................................................................................................

..........................................................................................................

Daily Intention or affirmation:

..........................................................................................................

..........................................................................................................

..........................................................................................................

# Evening

Good things that happened today

1. ..................................................................................................
   ..................................................................................................
2. ..................................................................................................
   ..................................................................................................
3. ..................................................................................................
   ..................................................................................................

Things I can do to make tomorrow better

1. ..................................................................................................
   ..................................................................................................
2. ..................................................................................................
   ..................................................................................................
3. ..................................................................................................
   ..................................................................................................

I showed myself love today by:

..........................................................................................................

..........................................................................................................

# Self-Check In

Date.........................................

How do I feel right now?

..........................................................................................................................

..........................................................................................................................

..........................................................................................................................

..........................................................................................................................

..........................................................................................................................

Why do I feel this way?

..........................................................................................................................

..........................................................................................................................

..........................................................................................................................

..........................................................................................................................

..........................................................................................................................

If the feeling is a positive one, what's one action I can take to enhance it or repeat it?

..........................................................................................................................

..........................................................................................................................

..........................................................................................................................

..........................................................................................................................

..........................................................................................................................

If the feeling is a negative one, what's one action I can take to improve my state, the situation, or raise my vibration?

..........................................................................................................................

..........................................................................................................................

..........................................................................................................................

..........................................................................................................................

..........................................................................................................................

# Morning

Date.......................................

I am grateful for:

.....................................................................................................

.....................................................................................................

.....................................................................................................

I'm looking forward to:

.....................................................................................................

.....................................................................................................

.....................................................................................................

Daily Intention or affirmation:

.....................................................................................................

.....................................................................................................

.....................................................................................................

# Evening

Good things that happened today

1. ............................................................................................

   ............................................................................................

2. ............................................................................................

   ............................................................................................

3. ............................................................................................

   ............................................................................................

Things I can do to make tomorrow better

1. ............................................................................................

   ............................................................................................

2. ............................................................................................

   ............................................................................................

3. ............................................................................................

   ............................................................................................

I showed myself love today by:

.....................................................................................................

.....................................................................................................

# Self-Check In

Date.......................................

How do I feel right now?

..................................................................................................

..................................................................................................

..................................................................................................

..................................................................................................

..................................................................................................

Why do I feel this way?

..................................................................................................

..................................................................................................

..................................................................................................

..................................................................................................

..................................................................................................

If the feeling is a positive one, what's one action I can take to enhance it or repeat it?

..................................................................................................

..................................................................................................

..................................................................................................

..................................................................................................

..................................................................................................

If the feeling is a negative one, what's one action I can take to improve my state, the situation, or raise my vibration?

..................................................................................................

..................................................................................................

..................................................................................................

..................................................................................................

..................................................................................................

# Morning

Date......................................

I am grateful for:

..............................................................................................................

..............................................................................................................

..............................................................................................................

I'm looking forward to:

..............................................................................................................

..............................................................................................................

..............................................................................................................

Daily Intention or affirmation:

..............................................................................................................

..............................................................................................................

..............................................................................................................

# Evening

Good things that happened today

1. ........................................................................................................
   ........................................................................................................
2. ........................................................................................................
   ........................................................................................................
3. ........................................................................................................
   ........................................................................................................

Things I can do to make tomorrow better

1. ........................................................................................................
   ........................................................................................................
2. ........................................................................................................
   ........................................................................................................
3. ........................................................................................................
   ........................................................................................................

I showed myself love today by:

..............................................................................................................

..............................................................................................................

# Self-Check In

Date......................................

How do I feel right now?

..........................................................................................

..........................................................................................

..........................................................................................

..........................................................................................

..........................................................................................

Why do I feel this way?

..........................................................................................

..........................................................................................

..........................................................................................

..........................................................................................

..........................................................................................

If the feeling is a positive one, what's one action I can take to enhance it or repeat it?

..........................................................................................

..........................................................................................

..........................................................................................

..........................................................................................

..........................................................................................

If the feeling is a negative one, what's one action I can take to improve my state, the situation, or raise my vibration?

..........................................................................................

..........................................................................................

..........................................................................................

..........................................................................................

..........................................................................................

# Morning

Date........................................

I am grateful for:

..................................................................................................

..................................................................................................

..................................................................................................

I'm looking forward to:

..................................................................................................

..................................................................................................

..................................................................................................

Daily Intention or affirmation:

..................................................................................................

..................................................................................................

..................................................................................................

# Evening

Good things that happened today

1. ...........................................................................................
   ...........................................................................................
2. ...........................................................................................
   ...........................................................................................
3. ...........................................................................................
   ...........................................................................................

Things I can do to make tomorrow better

1. ...........................................................................................
   ...........................................................................................
2. ...........................................................................................
   ...........................................................................................
3. ...........................................................................................
   ...........................................................................................

I showed myself love today by:

..................................................................................................

..................................................................................................

# Self-Check In

Date.......................................

How do I feel right now?

.................................................................................................................
.................................................................................................................
.................................................................................................................
.................................................................................................................
.................................................................................................................

Why do I feel this way?

.................................................................................................................
.................................................................................................................
.................................................................................................................
.................................................................................................................
.................................................................................................................

If the feeling is a positive one, what's one action I can take to enhance it or repeat it?

.................................................................................................................
.................................................................................................................
.................................................................................................................
.................................................................................................................
.................................................................................................................

If the feeling is a negative one, what's one action I can take to improve my state, the situation, or raise my vibration?

.................................................................................................................
.................................................................................................................
.................................................................................................................
.................................................................................................................
.................................................................................................................

# Morning

Date.......................................

I am grateful for:

....................................................................................................

....................................................................................................

....................................................................................................

I'm looking forward to:

....................................................................................................

....................................................................................................

....................................................................................................

Daily Intention or affirmation:

....................................................................................................

....................................................................................................

....................................................................................................

# Evening

Good things that happened today

1. ............................................................................................
   ............................................................................................
2. ............................................................................................
   ............................................................................................
3. ............................................................................................
   ............................................................................................

Things I can do to make tomorrow better

1. ............................................................................................
   ............................................................................................
2. ............................................................................................
   ............................................................................................
3. ............................................................................................
   ............................................................................................

I showed myself love today by:

....................................................................................................

....................................................................................................

# Self-Check In

Date.......................................

How do I feel right now?

.................................................................................................

.................................................................................................

.................................................................................................

.................................................................................................

.................................................................................................

Why do I feel this way?

.................................................................................................

.................................................................................................

.................................................................................................

.................................................................................................

.................................................................................................

If the feeling is a positive one, what's one action I can take to enhance it or repeat it?

.................................................................................................

.................................................................................................

.................................................................................................

.................................................................................................

.................................................................................................

If the feeling is a negative one, what's one action I can take to improve my state, the situation, or raise my vibration?

.................................................................................................

.................................................................................................

.................................................................................................

.................................................................................................

.................................................................................................

# Morning

Date......................................

I am grateful for:

..........................................................................................................
..........................................................................................................
..........................................................................................................

I'm looking forward to:

..........................................................................................................
..........................................................................................................
..........................................................................................................

Daily Intention or affirmation:

..........................................................................................................
..........................................................................................................
..........................................................................................................

# Evening

Good things that happened today

1. ..................................................................................................
   ..................................................................................................
2. ..................................................................................................
   ..................................................................................................
3. ..................................................................................................
   ..................................................................................................

Things I can do to make tomorrow better

1. ..................................................................................................
   ..................................................................................................
2. ..................................................................................................
   ..................................................................................................
3. ..................................................................................................
   ..................................................................................................

I showed myself love today by:

..........................................................................................................
..........................................................................................................

# Self-Check In

Date.......................................

How do I feel right now?

..........................................................................................................

..........................................................................................................

..........................................................................................................

..........................................................................................................

..........................................................................................................

Why do I feel this way?

..........................................................................................................

..........................................................................................................

..........................................................................................................

..........................................................................................................

..........................................................................................................

If the feeling is a positive one, what's one action I can take to enhance it or repeat it?

..........................................................................................................

..........................................................................................................

..........................................................................................................

..........................................................................................................

..........................................................................................................

If the feeling is a negative one, what's one action I can take to improve my state, the situation, or raise my vibration?

..........................................................................................................

..........................................................................................................

..........................................................................................................

..........................................................................................................

..........................................................................................................

# Morning

Date.........................................

I am grateful for:

..........................................................................................................

..........................................................................................................

..........................................................................................................

I'm looking forward to:

..........................................................................................................

..........................................................................................................

..........................................................................................................

Daily Intention or affirmation:

..........................................................................................................

..........................................................................................................

..........................................................................................................

# Evening

Good things that happened today

1. ..................................................................................................
   ..................................................................................................
2. ..................................................................................................
   ..................................................................................................
3. ..................................................................................................
   ..................................................................................................

Things I can do to make tomorrow better

1. ..................................................................................................
   ..................................................................................................
2. ..................................................................................................
   ..................................................................................................
3. ..................................................................................................
   ..................................................................................................

I showed myself love today by:

..........................................................................................................

..........................................................................................................

# Self-Check In

Date.......................................

How do I feel right now?

..........................................................................................................

..........................................................................................................

..........................................................................................................

..........................................................................................................

..........................................................................................................

Why do I feel this way?

..........................................................................................................

..........................................................................................................

..........................................................................................................

..........................................................................................................

..........................................................................................................

If the feeling is a positive one, what's one action I can take to enhance it or repeat it?

..........................................................................................................

..........................................................................................................

..........................................................................................................

..........................................................................................................

..........................................................................................................

If the feeling is a negative one, what's one action I can take to improve my state, the situation, or raise my vibration?

..........................................................................................................

..........................................................................................................

..........................................................................................................

..........................................................................................................

..........................................................................................................

# Morning

Date.......................................

I am grateful for:

..................................................................................................................

..................................................................................................................

..................................................................................................................

I'm looking forward to:

..................................................................................................................

..................................................................................................................

..................................................................................................................

Daily Intention or affirmation:

..................................................................................................................

..................................................................................................................

..................................................................................................................

# Evening

Good things that happened today

1. ..........................................................................................................
   ..........................................................................................................
2. ..........................................................................................................
   ..........................................................................................................
3. ..........................................................................................................
   ..........................................................................................................

Things I can do to make tomorrow better

1. ..........................................................................................................
   ..........................................................................................................
2. ..........................................................................................................
   ..........................................................................................................
3. ..........................................................................................................
   ..........................................................................................................

I showed myself love today by:

..................................................................................................................

..................................................................................................................

# Self-Check In

Date.......................................

How do I feel right now?

..........................................................................................................

..........................................................................................................

..........................................................................................................

..........................................................................................................

..........................................................................................................

Why do I feel this way?

..........................................................................................................

..........................................................................................................

..........................................................................................................

..........................................................................................................

..........................................................................................................

If the feeling is a positive one, what's one action I can take to enhance it or repeat it?

..........................................................................................................

..........................................................................................................

..........................................................................................................

..........................................................................................................

..........................................................................................................

If the feeling is a negative one, what's one action I can take to improve my state, the situation, or raise my vibration?

..........................................................................................................

..........................................................................................................

..........................................................................................................

..........................................................................................................

..........................................................................................................

# Morning

Date.......................................

I am grateful for:

.......................................................................................................

.......................................................................................................

.......................................................................................................

I'm looking forward to:

.......................................................................................................

.......................................................................................................

.......................................................................................................

Daily Intention or affirmation:

.......................................................................................................

.......................................................................................................

.......................................................................................................

# Evening

Good things that happened today

1. ..................................................................................................
   ..................................................................................................
2. ..................................................................................................
   ..................................................................................................
3. ..................................................................................................
   ..................................................................................................

Things I can do to make tomorrow better

1. ..................................................................................................
   ..................................................................................................
2. ..................................................................................................
   ..................................................................................................
3. ..................................................................................................
   ..................................................................................................

I showed myself love today by:

.......................................................................................................

.......................................................................................................

# Self-Check In

Date....................................

How do I feel right now?

..........................................................................................................

..........................................................................................................

..........................................................................................................

..........................................................................................................

..........................................................................................................

Why do I feel this way?

..........................................................................................................

..........................................................................................................

..........................................................................................................

..........................................................................................................

..........................................................................................................

If the feeling is a positive one, what's one action I can take to enhance it or repeat it?

..........................................................................................................

..........................................................................................................

..........................................................................................................

..........................................................................................................

..........................................................................................................

If the feeling is a negative one, what's one action I can take to improve my state, the situation, or raise my vibration?

..........................................................................................................

..........................................................................................................

..........................................................................................................

..........................................................................................................

..........................................................................................................

# Morning

Date.......................................

I am grateful for:

..........................................................................................................
..........................................................................................................
..........................................................................................................

I'm looking forward to:

..........................................................................................................
..........................................................................................................
..........................................................................................................

Daily Intention or affirmation:

..........................................................................................................
..........................................................................................................
..........................................................................................................

# Evening

Good things that happened today

1. ..................................................................................................
   ..................................................................................................
2. ..................................................................................................
   ..................................................................................................
3. ..................................................................................................
   ..................................................................................................

Things I can do to make tomorrow better

1. ..................................................................................................
   ..................................................................................................
2. ..................................................................................................
   ..................................................................................................
3. ..................................................................................................
   ..................................................................................................

I showed myself love today by:

..........................................................................................................
..........................................................................................................

# Self-Check In

Date....................................

How do I feel right now?

................................................................................................................

................................................................................................................

................................................................................................................

................................................................................................................

................................................................................................................

Why do I feel this way?

................................................................................................................

................................................................................................................

................................................................................................................

................................................................................................................

................................................................................................................

If the feeling is a positive one, what's one action I can take to enhance it or repeat it?

................................................................................................................

................................................................................................................

................................................................................................................

................................................................................................................

................................................................................................................

If the feeling is a negative one, what's one action I can take to improve my state, the situation, or raise my vibration?

................................................................................................................

................................................................................................................

................................................................................................................

................................................................................................................

................................................................................................................

# Morning

Date.......................................

I am grateful for:

..............................................................................................................

..............................................................................................................

..............................................................................................................

I'm looking forward to:

..............................................................................................................

..............................................................................................................

..............................................................................................................

Daily Intention or affirmation:

..............................................................................................................

..............................................................................................................

..............................................................................................................

# Evening

Good things that happened today

1. ......................................................................................................
   ......................................................................................................
2. ......................................................................................................
   ......................................................................................................
3. ......................................................................................................
   ......................................................................................................

Things I can do to make tomorrow better

1. ......................................................................................................
   ......................................................................................................
2. ......................................................................................................
   ......................................................................................................
3. ......................................................................................................
   ......................................................................................................

I showed myself love today by:

..............................................................................................................

..............................................................................................................

# Self-Check In

Date......................................

How do I feel right now?

..................................................................................................

..................................................................................................

..................................................................................................

..................................................................................................

..................................................................................................

Why do I feel this way?

..................................................................................................

..................................................................................................

..................................................................................................

..................................................................................................

..................................................................................................

If the feeling is a positive one, what's one action I can take to enhance it or repeat it?

..................................................................................................

..................................................................................................

..................................................................................................

..................................................................................................

..................................................................................................

If the feeling is a negative one, what's one action I can take to improve my state, the situation, or raise my vibration?

..................................................................................................

..................................................................................................

..................................................................................................

..................................................................................................

..................................................................................................

# Morning

Date......................................

I am grateful for:

..........................................................................................................

..........................................................................................................

..........................................................................................................

I'm looking forward to:

..........................................................................................................

..........................................................................................................

..........................................................................................................

Daily Intention or affirmation:

..........................................................................................................

..........................................................................................................

..........................................................................................................

# Evening

Good things that happened today

1. ..........................................................................................................
   ..........................................................................................................
2. ..........................................................................................................
   ..........................................................................................................
3. ..........................................................................................................
   ..........................................................................................................

Things I can do to make tomorrow better

1. ..........................................................................................................
   ..........................................................................................................
2. ..........................................................................................................
   ..........................................................................................................
3. ..........................................................................................................
   ..........................................................................................................

I showed myself love today by:

..........................................................................................................

..........................................................................................................

# Self-Check In

Date.......................................

How do I feel right now?

..................................................................................................

..................................................................................................

..................................................................................................

..................................................................................................

..................................................................................................

Why do I feel this way?

..................................................................................................

..................................................................................................

..................................................................................................

..................................................................................................

..................................................................................................

If the feeling is a positive one, what's one action I can take to enhance it or repeat it?

..................................................................................................

..................................................................................................

..................................................................................................

..................................................................................................

..................................................................................................

If the feeling is a negative one, what's one action I can take to improve my state, the situation, or raise my vibration?

..................................................................................................

..................................................................................................

..................................................................................................

..................................................................................................

..................................................................................................

# Morning

Date.......................................

I am grateful for:

..........................................................................................

..........................................................................................

..........................................................................................

I'm looking forward to:

..........................................................................................

..........................................................................................

..........................................................................................

Daily Intention or affirmation:

..........................................................................................

..........................................................................................

..........................................................................................

# Evening

Good things that happened today

1. ..........................................................................................
   ..........................................................................................
2. ..........................................................................................
   ..........................................................................................
3. ..........................................................................................
   ..........................................................................................

Things I can do to make tomorrow better

1. ..........................................................................................
   ..........................................................................................
2. ..........................................................................................
   ..........................................................................................
3. ..........................................................................................
   ..........................................................................................

I showed myself love today by:

..........................................................................................

..........................................................................................

# Self-Check In

Date.....................................

How do I feel right now?

..........................................................................................................

..........................................................................................................

..........................................................................................................

..........................................................................................................

..........................................................................................................

Why do I feel this way?

..........................................................................................................

..........................................................................................................

..........................................................................................................

..........................................................................................................

..........................................................................................................

If the feeling is a positive one, what's one action I can take to enhance it or repeat it?

..........................................................................................................

..........................................................................................................

..........................................................................................................

..........................................................................................................

..........................................................................................................

If the feeling is a negative one, what's one action I can take to improve my state, the situation, or raise my vibration?

..........................................................................................................

..........................................................................................................

..........................................................................................................

..........................................................................................................

..........................................................................................................

# Morning

Date.......................................

I am grateful for:

...............................................................................................................

...............................................................................................................

...............................................................................................................

I'm looking forward to:

...............................................................................................................

...............................................................................................................

...............................................................................................................

Daily Intention or affirmation:

...............................................................................................................

...............................................................................................................

...............................................................................................................

# Evening

Good things that happened today

1. ..........................................................................................................
   ..........................................................................................................
2. ..........................................................................................................
   ..........................................................................................................
3. ..........................................................................................................
   ..........................................................................................................

Things I can do to make tomorrow better

1. ..........................................................................................................
   ..........................................................................................................
2. ..........................................................................................................
   ..........................................................................................................
3. ..........................................................................................................
   ..........................................................................................................

I showed myself love today by:

...............................................................................................................

...............................................................................................................

# Self-Check In

Date........................................

How do I feel right now?

..........................................................................................................

..........................................................................................................

..........................................................................................................

..........................................................................................................

..........................................................................................................

Why do I feel this way?

..........................................................................................................

..........................................................................................................

..........................................................................................................

..........................................................................................................

..........................................................................................................

If the feeling is a positive one, what's one action I can take to enhance it or repeat it?

..........................................................................................................

..........................................................................................................

..........................................................................................................

..........................................................................................................

..........................................................................................................

If the feeling is a negative one, what's one action I can take to improve my state, the situation, or raise my vibration?

..........................................................................................................

..........................................................................................................

..........................................................................................................

..........................................................................................................

..........................................................................................................

# Morning

Date.......................................

I am grateful for:

..........................................................................................................

..........................................................................................................

..........................................................................................................

I'm looking forward to:

..........................................................................................................

..........................................................................................................

..........................................................................................................

Daily Intention or affirmation:

..........................................................................................................

..........................................................................................................

..........................................................................................................

# Evening

Good things that happened today

1. ..........................................................................................................
   ..........................................................................................................
2. ..........................................................................................................
   ..........................................................................................................
3. ..........................................................................................................
   ..........................................................................................................

Things I can do to make tomorrow better

1. ..........................................................................................................
   ..........................................................................................................
2. ..........................................................................................................
   ..........................................................................................................
3. ..........................................................................................................
   ..........................................................................................................

I showed myself love today by:

..........................................................................................................

..........................................................................................................

# Self-Check In

Date.......................................

How do I feel right now?

.......................................................................................................

.......................................................................................................

.......................................................................................................

.......................................................................................................

.......................................................................................................

Why do I feel this way?

.......................................................................................................

.......................................................................................................

.......................................................................................................

.......................................................................................................

.......................................................................................................

If the feeling is a positive one, what's one action I can take to enhance it or repeat it?

.......................................................................................................

.......................................................................................................

.......................................................................................................

.......................................................................................................

.......................................................................................................

If the feeling is a negative one, what's one action I can take to improve my state, the situation, or raise my vibration?

.......................................................................................................

.......................................................................................................

.......................................................................................................

.......................................................................................................

.......................................................................................................

## Morning

Date.........................................

I am grateful for:

..........................................................................................................

..........................................................................................................

..........................................................................................................

I'm looking forward to:

..........................................................................................................

..........................................................................................................

..........................................................................................................

Daily Intention or affirmation:

..........................................................................................................

..........................................................................................................

..........................................................................................................

## Evening

Good things that happened today

1. ..........................................................................................................
   ..........................................................................................................
2. ..........................................................................................................
   ..........................................................................................................
3. ..........................................................................................................
   ..........................................................................................................

Things I can do to make tomorrow better

1. ..........................................................................................................
   ..........................................................................................................
2. ..........................................................................................................
   ..........................................................................................................
3. ..........................................................................................................
   ..........................................................................................................

I showed myself love today by:

..........................................................................................................

..........................................................................................................

# Self-Check In

Date......................................

How do I feel right now?

..........................................................................................................

..........................................................................................................

..........................................................................................................

..........................................................................................................

..........................................................................................................

Why do I feel this way?

..........................................................................................................

..........................................................................................................

..........................................................................................................

..........................................................................................................

..........................................................................................................

If the feeling is a positive one, what's one action I can take to enhance it or repeat it?

..........................................................................................................

..........................................................................................................

..........................................................................................................

..........................................................................................................

..........................................................................................................

If the feeling is a negative one, what's one action I can take to improve my state, the situation, or raise my vibration?

..........................................................................................................

..........................................................................................................

..........................................................................................................

..........................................................................................................

..........................................................................................................

# Morning

Date....................................

I am grateful for:

.................................................................................................................
.................................................................................................................
.................................................................................................................

I'm looking forward to:

.................................................................................................................
.................................................................................................................
.................................................................................................................

Daily Intention or affirmation:

.................................................................................................................
.................................................................................................................
.................................................................................................................

# Evening

Good things that happened today

1. .........................................................................................................
   .........................................................................................................
2. .........................................................................................................
   .........................................................................................................
3. .........................................................................................................
   .........................................................................................................

Things I can do to make tomorrow better

1. .........................................................................................................
   .........................................................................................................
2. .........................................................................................................
   .........................................................................................................
3. .........................................................................................................
   .........................................................................................................

I showed myself love today by:

.................................................................................................................
.................................................................................................................

# Self-Check In

Date......................................

How do I feel right now?

.........................................................................................................

.........................................................................................................

.........................................................................................................

.........................................................................................................

.........................................................................................................

Why do I feel this way?

.........................................................................................................

.........................................................................................................

.........................................................................................................

.........................................................................................................

.........................................................................................................

If the feeling is a positive one, what's one action I can take to enhance it or repeat it?

.........................................................................................................

.........................................................................................................

.........................................................................................................

.........................................................................................................

.........................................................................................................

If the feeling is a negative one, what's one action I can take to improve my state, the situation, or raise my vibration?

.........................................................................................................

.........................................................................................................

.........................................................................................................

.........................................................................................................

.........................................................................................................

# Morning

Date....................................

I am grateful for:

........................................................................................................................

........................................................................................................................

........................................................................................................................

I'm looking forward to:

........................................................................................................................

........................................................................................................................

........................................................................................................................

Daily Intention or affirmation:

........................................................................................................................

........................................................................................................................

........................................................................................................................

# Evening

Good things that happened today

1. ..................................................................................................................
   ..................................................................................................................
2. ..................................................................................................................
   ..................................................................................................................
3. ..................................................................................................................
   ..................................................................................................................

Things I can do to make tomorrow better

1. ..................................................................................................................
   ..................................................................................................................
2. ..................................................................................................................
   ..................................................................................................................
3. ..................................................................................................................
   ..................................................................................................................

I showed myself love today by:

........................................................................................................................

........................................................................................................................

# Self-Check In

Date.......................................

How do I feel right now?

..........................................................................................................................

..........................................................................................................................

..........................................................................................................................

..........................................................................................................................

..........................................................................................................................

Why do I feel this way?

..........................................................................................................................

..........................................................................................................................

..........................................................................................................................

..........................................................................................................................

..........................................................................................................................

If the feeling is a positive one, what's one action I can take to enhance it or repeat it?

..........................................................................................................................

..........................................................................................................................

..........................................................................................................................

..........................................................................................................................

..........................................................................................................................

If the feeling is a negative one, what's one action I can take to improve my state, the situation, or raise my vibration?

..........................................................................................................................

..........................................................................................................................

..........................................................................................................................

..........................................................................................................................

..........................................................................................................................

# Morning

Date.......................................

I am grateful for:

........................................................................................................................
........................................................................................................................
........................................................................................................................

I'm looking forward to:

........................................................................................................................
........................................................................................................................
........................................................................................................................

Daily Intention or affirmation:

........................................................................................................................
........................................................................................................................
........................................................................................................................

# Evening

Good things that happened today

1. ..................................................................................................................
   ..................................................................................................................
2. ..................................................................................................................
   ..................................................................................................................
3. ..................................................................................................................
   ..................................................................................................................

Things I can do to make tomorrow better

1. ..................................................................................................................
   ..................................................................................................................
2. ..................................................................................................................
   ..................................................................................................................
3. ..................................................................................................................
   ..................................................................................................................

I showed myself love today by:

........................................................................................................................
........................................................................................................................

# Self-Check In

Date........................................

How do I feel right now?

..........................................................................................................

..........................................................................................................

..........................................................................................................

..........................................................................................................

..........................................................................................................

Why do I feel this way?

..........................................................................................................

..........................................................................................................

..........................................................................................................

..........................................................................................................

..........................................................................................................

If the feeling is a positive one, what's one action I can take to enhance it or repeat it?

..........................................................................................................

..........................................................................................................

..........................................................................................................

..........................................................................................................

..........................................................................................................

If the feeling is a negative one, what's one action I can take to improve my state, the situation, or raise my vibration?

..........................................................................................................

..........................................................................................................

..........................................................................................................

..........................................................................................................

..........................................................................................................

# Morning

Date......................................

I am grateful for:

...............................................................................................................

...............................................................................................................

...............................................................................................................

I'm looking forward to:

...............................................................................................................

...............................................................................................................

...............................................................................................................

Daily Intention or affirmation:

...............................................................................................................

...............................................................................................................

...............................................................................................................

# Evening

Good things that happened today

1. .........................................................................................................
   .........................................................................................................
2. .........................................................................................................
   .........................................................................................................
3. .........................................................................................................
   .........................................................................................................

Things I can do to make tomorrow better

1. .........................................................................................................
   .........................................................................................................
2. .........................................................................................................
   .........................................................................................................
3. .........................................................................................................
   .........................................................................................................

I showed myself love today by:

...............................................................................................................

...............................................................................................................

# Self-Check In

Date.......................................

How do I feel right now?

..........................................................................................................

..........................................................................................................

..........................................................................................................

..........................................................................................................

..........................................................................................................

Why do I feel this way?

..........................................................................................................

..........................................................................................................

..........................................................................................................

..........................................................................................................

..........................................................................................................

If the feeling is a positive one, what's one action I can take to enhance it or repeat it?

..........................................................................................................

..........................................................................................................

..........................................................................................................

..........................................................................................................

..........................................................................................................

If the feeling is a negative one, what's one action I can take to improve my state, the situation, or raise my vibration?

..........................................................................................................

..........................................................................................................

..........................................................................................................

..........................................................................................................

..........................................................................................................

# Morning

Date.......................................

I am grateful for:

.....................................................................................................
.....................................................................................................
.....................................................................................................

I'm looking forward to:

.....................................................................................................
.....................................................................................................
.....................................................................................................

Daily Intention or affirmation:

.....................................................................................................
.....................................................................................................
.....................................................................................................

# Evening

Good things that happened today

1. ...............................................................................................
   ...............................................................................................
2. ...............................................................................................
   ...............................................................................................
3. ...............................................................................................
   ...............................................................................................

Things I can do to make tomorrow better

1. ...............................................................................................
   ...............................................................................................
2. ...............................................................................................
   ...............................................................................................
3. ...............................................................................................
   ...............................................................................................

I showed myself love today by:

.....................................................................................................
.....................................................................................................

# Self-Check In

Date.........................................

How do I feel right now?

..........................................................................................................................

..........................................................................................................................

..........................................................................................................................

..........................................................................................................................

..........................................................................................................................

Why do I feel this way?

..........................................................................................................................

..........................................................................................................................

..........................................................................................................................

..........................................................................................................................

..........................................................................................................................

If the feeling is a positive one, what's one action I can take to enhance it or repeat it?

..........................................................................................................................

..........................................................................................................................

..........................................................................................................................

..........................................................................................................................

..........................................................................................................................

If the feeling is a negative one, what's one action I can take to improve my state, the situation, or raise my vibration?

..........................................................................................................................

..........................................................................................................................

..........................................................................................................................

..........................................................................................................................

..........................................................................................................................

www.ingramcontent.com/pod-product-compliance
Lightning Source LLC
Chambersburg PA
CBHW070822020826
48982CB00014B/202

* 9 7 8 1 7 3 3 6 4 1 9 7 5 *